A Swim Story

The true untold story of the sexual
abuse of one of Eastern Europe's
most successful female swim teams

by
Ross C. Hack

Bloomington, IN   Milton Keynes, UK

AuthorHouse™
1663 Liberty Drive, Suite 200
Bloomington, IN 47403
www.authorhouse.com
Phone: 1-800-839-8640

AuthorHouse™ UK Ltd.
500 Avebury Boulevard
Central Milton Keynes, MK9 2BE
www.authorhouse.co.uk
Phone: 08001974150

This book is a work of non-fiction. Unless otherwise noted, the author and the publisher make no explicit guarantees as to the accuracy of the information contained in this book and in some cases, names of people and places have been altered to protect their privacy.

First published by AuthorHouse 6/5/2007

ISBN: 978-1-4259-9323-8 (sc)

Printed in the United States of America
Bloomington, Indiana

This book is printed on acid-free paper.

My thanks for their help and support to get this story in print goes out to three people – "Anna" who is the real hero of this story, Jonathan Finch for his unending support, criticism, wisdom, and friendship, and "Jeremy McKinnon" who tried what he could to help.

Table of Contents

Part 1

Part 2

Part 1

Introduction

Imagine as an American Parent you have a daughter involved in a sport—a sport she loves. For her it's a chance to be someone more, increase self-esteem, and possibly to accomplish goals that are out of the reach of most people. She is good—better than most—and motivated. She begins to envision herself as a future recognized sports star. She applies herself to this dream and trains even harder. As a parent you are proud she is giving an effort that most will not, and you are happy she is blessed with the ability to strive harder and focus on her goals. Now imagine that your daughter, after years of dedicating her life to this sport, comes home one day and tells you that she has had enough. Now, for a young lady who gave her all and did not excel past her peers, one with the strength to admit that the tools that nature and nurture have given her just aren't enough to beat the better ones, her parents would express understanding and just be happy that their daughter gave it her best, tried, and had fun doing it. But what about the parent who has a daughter who surpasses most of her peers in the sport; a daughter who is presently one of a few above the rest; one who is still young and knows she still has yet to reach her potential; a daughter who has won many competitions, broken national records, traveled and represented not only the family name, but represented a whole nation? What if you had such a daughter who came home one day and said, "I'm finished"? A parent would be confused. Why? Why now, when your young daughters' dreams were not fully realized and yet only a short distant away? Surely she is physically able and still yet to reach her physical zenith. She could not quit after going so far. There are more victories that lay ahead, more people and places in the world to see. She is gifted to be able to achieve such esteemed dreams already. Other girls only have the ability to dream about such achievements while your daughter is living them. So why does she want to stop competing now?

As a parent, this is a time to sit with your daughter; a time to come to an understanding of why she made such a decision. What are her reasons when there are obvious signs of future success—signs that show she could be further recognized for her efforts; signs that could greatly increase her chances for living a more comfortable life than her parents and grandparents. Maybe you could persuade your daughter not to quit. Maybe after talking with her you will realize that some smaller trial of life is affecting her decision. Knowing you're a good parent, you could give her the support, experience, and advice she needs to put her mentally back on track.

As your daughter sits with you and builds the strength to discuss the reasons to call it quits you realize her sadness is not that of just mourning the passing of a happy era in her life, but passing an era of great distress. Imagine that what you hear from your daughter are not the reasons one would expect, especially now that she is a respected world-class athlete. You are shocked and horrified by what she tells you. This causes disbelief which quickly turns into anger—anger that makes any American parent want to take immediate action, because such reasons, if true, would have the support and confidence of the community, nation, and ethical and judicial law.

What your daughter tells you is that she was abused sexually, mentally, and physically by her coach. She was not just abused yesterday but for the last seven years of her sports career, since the age of 13. You are shocked to learn this now after so long. Why didn't you know about this earlier? That's not all. She tells you it has happened and is happening now to many other girls on her team.

As an American you know the implications of child sexual abuse, especially for those in positions of power and influence who have built the child's trust and confidence. As a parent those sexual and physical abuse cases from the television and newspapers have a new, profound effect. It is now happening to you and your child. The action for an American is almost natural: calling family and friends while holding back thoughts of taking vengeance personally in the most extreme ways. Being civilized, you will wait a moment then call the police, with the protection of your child and the children of others in mind. Ultimately, you want the most severe form of justice to be taken against the perpetrator.

You now look at your daughter with no thought of her returning to such an environment of abuse. How could you have not known what she was going through for so long? How could it have existed without the actions or at least knowledge of others since your daughter was competing at a national, world and even Olympic level? You may blame yourself. Did you not see any signs of this? Did your daughter give hints or say things that you just blew off? As an American you are at least confident that justice will be served at the community, local, and federal level. But, what if you are someone else—not an American, but someone living in a country where people have less confidence that justice can be carried out in such matters?

Most of us could probably believe there are countries where parents have little confidence that justice will be served to those who commit crimes of sexual, physical, and mental abuse against their children. For me, the author of this book, I know there is one country like this. It is not a small, poor, third-world one tucked away somewhere in Africa or Latin America. It is an industrial, powerful one with history far greater than our own. One that is well known, in the news almost daily, and has brought forth many great scientists, statesmen, inventors, dancers, musicians, writers, athletes, etc.

I came across this story in the summer of 2002 when I lived in Europe. During the six years I was there, I enjoyed listening in the many pubs and cafés the stories of those who traveled through Prague, the capital city of the Czech Republic, where I lived and went to college. If I wasn't in school or at the gym I was usually at one of Prague's many pubs or cafés. My favorites were the old wood-and-brick ones beneath the buildings that had the old-world look that unfortunately many times came with the old-world service mixed in with the bitter post-communist attitude. One summer afternoon I sat down in one of these pubs next to a beautiful lady. I asked her if she was in Prague on vacation as I could see she wasn't Czech. Her name was Anna and she was here on a two-week vacation. We accepted each other's hospitality to have a friendly chat over a few beers. In fact, a beer or three in the afternoon is a large part of the Czech culture. We ordered up a half liter each of some of the world's best beer—two *Staropramens*, a name that means "Old Water Spring." It was a Thursday around 5 p.m. The pub was filling up quickly as the locals got off work and out of school. Amongst the patrons' lively talk and loud jukebox in the background, we got to know each other while sitting across from one another on a heavy, wood table in a corner across from a staircase. It was hard to hear sometimes, as the pub's second floor, just above us, was filled with students always breaking out in loud laughter and shouting. Anna was not Czech, and conversed in broken English. We went through the usual questions of where we come from and why we're here. After a couple of beers and great Czech-style kung-pao chicken, she said that she used to be a swimmer.

I thought possibly I was going to hear another story of how someone could have gone big-time if it wasn't for some trial in life that held them back. No, that wasn't the case this time. With a bit of a modest grin she told me of her national records along with her many world-class medals and even competing in the Olympics. I had never even seen an Olympian in real life and now I was having the pleasure of enjoying dinner and a few drinks with one. For that matter, one who still looked in competition-form. She was in her twenties, and I asked if she would compete anymore.

"I thought about it but I doubt ever again, at least not in my country," Anna said. I asked why not, and she said her coach is horrible and treats her badly. I heard about bad treatment in some of the Soviet countries, and didn't think much more on the matter. What I found puzzling was that when Anna was at her peak at the young age of 19, she left the team. That was just after she went to the Olympics, broke national records, and became one of the world's top swimmers. I asked myself why she ended her career so soon. Who would leave their sport when they're so good and so young? Anna told me she now worked as a fitness instructor and also taught young children dance only making about $200 a month. There was something more to this, but I didn't know her well enough to ask things too personal.

We left the pub at the right time since the smoking of the locals was starting to burn our eyes; older places there usually don't have systems to clear the air. So I walked with her a bit outside in the warmth of a June night before I went to my small studio apartment. I guess I made a good enough impression, or at least was at the right place at the right time. She had just landed a few hours before and I was the first guy she really met. Before I left, I asked her if she would like me to show her around Prague since I had come to know it quite well. She agreed, and we found ourselves early the next morning sitting on the stone surrounding the statue of Jan Hus on Stare Mesto Namesti, which means "Old Town Square."

It was fun showing Anna around. As beautiful as Anna was she was a casual and simple lady who seemed to base her appearance on her natural beauty rather than trying to overcompensate with make-up, nail polish and the like. She wore her long blonde hair in a simple ponytail and walked around in the only sports shoes she owned. Strolling through Prague's center, we started asking more personal questions since we seemed to be in the feeling-out process of how much deeper we wanted to know each other. After the usual questions of family, likes and dislikes, etc., I could not help but ask her more about her unusual, short swimming career. While over a sundae at a small ice cream bar near the huge, shiny, silver, soviet-built communication tower in Zhishkov, I asked her again about leaving her team. She looked at me with a bit of anger: "my coach tried to have sex with me." I jokingly said, "I would have too," as to comment on her beauty. "He's a pig and I can't be around him anymore," she said. I really thought she was exaggerating.

I asked more details and she felt I had a sincere interest, rather than just being a passive listener making small talk. She mentioned that her coach tried to have sex with all his swimmers and beat them as well. She was obviously moved every time she talked about this, as her tone of voice and expressions gave me the feeling that she was quite heated over the matter.

There came an obvious point where Anna was excited that someone was listening to her story, as if I was the only one that ever cared. My interest was caught, as the more specific she became the more unnerving it was. She stated not only that her coach was abusive in more ways than one, but he had been abusive since they were very young. The story now delved into the arena of child molestation, pedophilia, coercion, and mental and sexual abuse. I became really concerned not because of what the coach had done, but because, according to Anna, the coach was still coaching. How could this be so if what Anna was saying was true? In the next few days I heard more and more of Anna's story, and I began to get a better idea of what happened to her and her team. Anna said the worst part of it all was that since he was the coach no one could do anything about it, because all the young girls were too afraid, embarrassed, and felt they had no one to turn to for help.

She explained to me in detail many things that I find beyond impossible if it had happened in America. Of course, Americans have been exposed to many stories about such abuses and scandals. Though justice seems to be properly carried out in most cases, there are those stories that lead some to feel that the abuser, pedophile, or molester could have been punished more or less. But, when no one makes an effort to expose these people, how can justice be carried out at all? How can justice be carried out in a system that has not protected a child in the first place? How can justice be carried out when those who do act have their complaints and accusations fall upon deaf ears? This is just the case of Anna and her country's most successful female national swim team.

I have mentioned many times throughout the introduction thus far the need for the reader to put himself or herself in the mindset of an American since it is written with an American audience in mind, but my motive is for these written words to be read not only by Americans, but also by those in the country where these abuses have been and are currently taking place. I mainly intend for this book to be read by those who have the authority and responsibility to protect and carry out justice that is expected by any citizen of a civilized nation. My overall purpose is for the girls who have been and are still being abused by their coach to have the confidence and courage to tell others what they have experienced. The only way they can do this is if they are confident that their community and country can protect them. This is not just for the girls who were part of Anna's swim team, but also for those children who have suffered similar and worse abuse because there are no willing state and government agencies, if they even exist, that support and protect children after they expose the abuse and abuser. With this in mind, my greatest hope is for this story to reach the proper levels of Anna's government to help influence it to take action and create a structure so that young boys and girls can feel safe, protected, and confident to expose their abusers; a structure that not only protects children, but also one that takes just action against and deters those would-be abusers. I don't see such a structure now, and most important of all, I don't see one that has the confidence of its people.

If such behavior and abuse can happen within this country's most successful female swim team, which had swimmers who won national, world, and Olympic medals; swimmers who hold swimming records today, then such behavior can surely exist in any other part of this society at levels that receive far less attention. Can we imagine this happening in a country like the United States? What if there were years of ongoing physical and sexual abuse by a coach on the United States Olympic Swim Team of his young, prepubescent and teenage female swimmers? There is no doubt what kind of publicity and public reaction this would cause. Americans would not even understand how sportswomen at such a high level who are carrying the respect and pride of their nation could have been abused for so long without anyone knowing or doing something about it. But, starting in 1990 in the large city of a former Soviet country where Anna is from, this is exactly what happened to a handful of girls who only had the hope of becoming champion swimmers and to create a better life for themselves. The following story is from my own investigation and extensive contact with Anna.

1

In the Beginning (1984)

In 1984 a man entered an elementary school of a large, industrial, darkened city many miles from the nation's capital. Anna remembers: "Ezra came into my classroom to find children he thought would make good swimmers. I was 7 years old. It was the first time I met my coach. He looked over all the kids and took measurements of our arms, legs, and waists. He tested how flexible and strong we were by asking us to perform small exercises. He was also looking for thin, taller children which have more of an advantage in swimming competitions. To those he thought would make good swimmers he gave a note. If the child wanted to be trained to swim their parents would have to allow them by signing and bringing the note back. Of course, all the kids who got such a note were very excited and rushed home to show their parents. This was like a ticket to do something more. Something more is what all the kids wanted. Sports were a ticket to meet new people and visit new places. Most of all, you could make life easier if you were successful".

Anna's city of 1984 was very much as it is today. It was an industrial city with a population over one million. The Bolsheviks changed the name when they occupied the region, but after the fall of Communism the city took back its original one. It is located less than one hundred miles northeast of the capital. At that time in 1984 it was a closed city, meaning that it was not open to any foreigners traveling in the Soviet Union. The city still has a huge military program for making and testing advanced technology. Jet engines, railroad equipment, chemicals, and machinery are also produced there. It is a river port city with its pleasant waters running directly through the center. Small freshwater fishing boats line the docks just south of the city center, where an old, stone bridge stands nearby, decorated with statues in Christian motifs. The Communist-era train station, which is a major hub for the lumber companies and transfers millions of tons of pine from the southern part of the province, is gray, bland, and in need of repairs and a paint job, but this is how life is brought to the city. The train is the major connection to the rest of the world. There is no airport, and the only planes seen are from the military testing grounds about 25 miles southwest of town.

1984 was also a time of Communism that was quickly moving towards collapse. One would not think to say that Anna's country in this year was a first-world nation. Streets and buildings were in much need of repair. Utilities such as water, electricity, heating, and telephone service were in bad shape. People littered without a conscience. There were open sewage holes where the inattentive could fall. Food shortages hit every so often, and street lights were not even common for many major roads. Violent crime was no where near American levels, but alcoholism for men was especially high. There is little in Anna's city that attracted the eye besides the young women taking in the warm summer sun when they were able to shed the heavy, wool coats from the long winters. One day in 1984, it was a chilly fall afternoon as Anna ran to the bus which would take her home from school so she could show her mom the note some swimming trainer gave her in class today.

Anna was very excited and very much wanted to swim. She could even get out of some classes once per week in order to train. But, when she came home to show her mother the note and explain the visit by Ezra, her mother said, "No."

"Why," Anna said.

"Because you already have piano lessons, gymnastics, dance, and good grades," Mariana, her mother, said.

Her mother Mariana was a short, dark-haired, wide-eyed lady who was quite an athlete in her younger age. Mariana had been divorced from Anna's father five years earlier. Anna's parents actually separated and lived apart when she was only two years old.

Anna's schedule was already packed with so much. She had to be up at six in the morning for school, and after going to her other activities she would not come home until 8:00 p.m., and then she would have to do homework, not going to sleep until ten or eleven. With this daily routine it was impossible for a little girl to do anything more.

That night Anna begged her mother to allow her to swim. She was happy when her mother finally gave in. They worked out a deal to reduce time spent in other activities. In a few years, Mariana would see that letting her daughter swim would answer her hopes of bearing a great athlete.

When Mariana was pregnant with her first and only child, Anna, she very much wanted her to be a successful athlete. "I would place my hands on my belly and say 'I know you will be a sportsman.' With Anna being so skinny I thought she would have been a gymnast, but she liked swimming so much...and see what happened," Mariana.

When Anna started swimming she was living with her mother and her mother's aunt, Lydie. They were living in Lydie's apartment which was located near the city center, just far enough away from the fishing docks to elude the smell. It was one of the better apartments in town, and it had just been renovated by the city. It was a three-story, typical, communist-style apartment building with elderly tenants always hanging around the entrance chatting up the gossip and playing chess. Anna described Lydie's place as cozy and always filled with goodies waiting just for her. The love and care that Anna's Great-Aunt Lydie gave them is the reason Anna always called her Grandma.

Lydie's home was not their real home. Their real home was the classic, gray, ten-story, soviet-style apartment building which was not aestheti-cally pleasing. It was located on Afinska Street, about one and one-half hours away by bus toward the east part of town near the old vegetable can-nery. Lydie's apartment made it easier for Anna and her mother to do the things they needed to do. It was much closer to all Anna's sports facili-ties, activities, and School #5, which she attended. Mariana worked as a secretary in a small univer-sity that was down the street from Lydie's. If they lived in their own apartment on Afinska Street it would not have allowed Mariana to make it on time for work while shuttling little Anna back and forth from School #5 and all her other activities. They didn't have a car nor did her mother ever learn how to drive.

2

Creating the Team (1985)

Ezra began to dream of coaching a swim team soon after he realized that his own vision of becoming a swimmer would never be actualized. Ezra was born in 1960 and never considered himself a swimmer. He was from a city in the southern part of the country where they built a swimming pool too late for him to start at the young age most coaches required. Ezra tells: "I started late swimming and coaches didn't want me when I was a small boy so I went into diving. Then I tried to move into swimming again later but had no past swimming career, and there were already a lot of swimmers at the time". Though the opportunity would not arise for a long while, it was at this time that he decided to be a swimming coach; for the time being, he just carried on wherever his life took him. He went on to finish up his schooling, obtaining a higher education in geology. He later studied geothermal energy at a school in the country's capital, and worked one year in the country's mining province as a land surveyor. Ezra goes on to say "...later after this I went crazy to have a swimming team. First I tried to get into a national sports university but didn't have the proper requisites to be accepted." This didn't stop him on his quest. One year later he moved back to the capital and finished a sports diploma in the National Sports University. With this he earned the credibility to be a potential coach. Now he had the basis needed, and it was time for him to decide where to find a team.

For his own reasons he settled on the idea of a city in the north where the fresher air from the forest region away from the polluted air of the capital made stronger, healthier swimmers. With such specs in mind, Anna's city was a perfect choice. Here he approached the government sports club of KA-14, which had a very nice swimming facility next to the river. With the city's school administration helping by allowing him to look for potential team members, he was on his way to finding a team. Ezra remembers: "I chose the best children, all girls the same age that were born in 1977 [seven-year-olds]. I looked at about 3000 girls. For the girl to be a good swimmer, she had to be tall, float good, thin bones, wide shoulders, narrow hips, flexible, etc."

It takes years to narrow down a team of potential competitive swimmers. Some of the girls who do not show promise at a young age could become the best swimmers when their bodies start to develop later. From the 3000 or so he examined, he chose one hundred girls. Anna was one of them. After basic training and the establishment of solid fundamentals, he reduced the team to the fifteen girls he thought had the best potential, and again Anna was chosen.

As Ezra whittled the team down to those he thought had a chance of success, he stepped up his training regimen. Naturally, due to this Anna slowly decreased all her former pursuits as swim training increased. Within three years, training went from once per week to a more focused schedule of three times per day. "It was a tough schedule but everyone who swam enjoyed it," Anna recalls. By the time Anna reached her third class in 1987 at the age of ten, she completely dropped all other activities so she could concentrate on swimming. "I loved it and only wanted to swim," Anna. She goes on, "I was in my fourth class at the age of eleven in 1988. Coach Ezra said that all the members of his team that are serious about swimming must now go to School #8. It was located right next door to our training center, KA-14."

School #8 was a normal, state-operated school, but Ezra worked out an arrangement where #8 would become an official, state-recognized sports school. Ezra and the school created a new student program called Class S. Class S accommodated the new, arriving potential athletes. Basically, it was designed to have a few physical education classes per day set aside for the students to attend their sports training sessions; and with the training center so close, the kids could walk to and from school a few times daily.

The army training center of KA-14 was a recently made, Olympic-style swimming facility. The pool itself was miles away from the rest of the army's training grounds. It would become the team's home and an ideal place for training during the Communist era. It was built in a nice location just down from National Square on the bank of the local river. On National Square sat the capitol building of the whole region. Built later in the nineties near KA-14 was the beautiful Christian Church of Saint Paul with its Byzantine-style architecture and golden domes. Between the church and KA-14 was the Undying Flame monument, which was dedicated to the soldiers who died in World War Two and depicted a soldier holding a torch that continuously burned with a real fire. Looking from the swimming pool across the river, you could see forests which could be reached by ferry until the long winter came, at which point you had to walk across the thick, frozen river surface. In the warmer season, the two-kilometer walk that began outside the west exit of KA-14 was filled with small cafés, food and ice cream stands, outdoor discos, and many visiting people who were taking advantage of the sun and warm beach below the walk. In all, it was the most scenic part of Anna's city, and a good place for a training center that would inspire its swimmers.

KA-14 itself was more than just an Olympic-style pool. It was a complex that had rooms much like those in a motel. The rooms were used by various people; those who didn't go home after training because they were too tired, young swimmers with parents who were out of town, those who just came to town and didn't have housing yet, or for those who just felt like staying the night and didn't want to make the long bus ride home just to come back the next morning.

Until now, coach Ezra did well organizing his fledgling swimmers by taking the necessary step of acquiring the proper resources such as a school with a training facility right next door to it. Anna said: "Most students left their former schools to attend School #8. Having the invitation improved their self-esteem since they were now being recognized more as a serious swimmer just for attending. I already felt pretty good about swimming since I came in fourth place in a competition among my team. This wasn't much, but I felt I would do better. On top of everything else, why wouldn't you move to a new school and carry on your training since it was a real chance to improve your life?"

3

Becoming a Team and Just Swimming

For the team members, life was all about swimming and trying to be the young girls they were. I asked Anna to describe her team and Ezra up to the age of when she was twelve: "When I first saw Ezra, he was an ideal sportsman. He was good looking, healthy and fit, and didn't show any signs of bad habits. I never had a father I could remember. My mother had to take care of me alone and couldn't work for the first ten months of my life. My father wasn't using his money to take care of the family and this problem was the cause of my parents' divorce. He stayed with my mother till she could go back to work after recovering from pregnancy, but then left us soon after. This was very hard on my mother and she was only making the equivalent of $90 a month, which was very little, but enough to live on at the time. So there was no father for financial support and my mother had very little free time to relax.

When I saw Ezra and got the invitation to become a member of the team, I was very excited. Never having a dad around growing up giving you attention I came to see him like a father within the first year of training. Many girls on the team didn't have fathers, and they felt the same way as me. He was really respected in the beginning. The team bonded into a group of friends since we saw each other more than anyone else. I made many friends like Blanka, Eliska, and Nicole. Blanka and Eliska I'm still good friends with, and see a lot when I visit home."

Red-haired and chubby-cheeked Blanka was much like Eliska and Anna. They all were born and grew up in this city, but Nicole was somewhat of a different class. Anna says, "Nicole became the most successful of our team. I met her in 1985, the first year of my training. I remember how the team was a bit jealous because she was the best off out of the team. She had the richest parents who both were chemists. When we first saw her she was wearing all new clothes which only came from outside the country. You only saw these clothes on TV." Nicole's swimming ability was discovered while swimming at a public pool in Serbia where her parents lived. Living in Serbia she had access to goods that others in a closed Soviet country didn't.

"She was very athletic, and proved to be one of the best of the team. I was also one of the best, and competition built between us. I remember in school when we had sporting competitions. She was always the captain of one side, and I was always the captain of the other. Whether it was basketball, soccer, or relay races, we were usually the captains competing against one another."

With most of Anna's time spent at the pool and school which were now right next to each other, her mother finally had time to herself and felt she and Anna could return to their real apartment on Afinska Street. Anna was sad to leave her aunt Lydie's home, but she decided to visit her on the weekends when she had time. "Grandma Lydie eventually moved out and into an apartment of a middle aged couple that promised to take care of her in exchange for most of her pension since old age was starting to slow her down," Anna later recounted. This would be a grave mistake for her aunt and one of the saddest points in Anna's life.

But it was all about the team now. The focus of her life became swimming. They would train a few times per day, laps upon laps, competing with each other and playing the games girls play. The team of 15 developed into a cohesive unit that worked much like a family. They trained and lived with each other more than they did with anyone else, including their parents. When training was hard and called for them to return early the next morning, they even had the opportunity to stay in a room at KA-14. Now, with the respect the girls had for Ezra, and with Ezra's confidence in developing a few competitive swimmers, it was time to prepare the team for the next level of training.

4

Becoming Someone and Training Psychology (1989)

The girls entered their first major event around age twelve. This was a nationally recognized event which carried some prestige. The team would soon find out their dedication to training would show in their results. The coach and his swimmers were nervous, as bad results could be very demoralizing, and could also mean the need to start a new strategy of training from scratch. However, this would not be the case.

This competition was held in the capital in 1989. Anna remembers: "I felt I was entering the competition as just another competitor. Nobody knew I would have done so good, including me and Ezra." She came in first place among most of the nations top competitors. She went on, "I was so happy that I couldn't really believe out of all the competitors in my country that I came in first at 12 years old. My mother was so surprised after she heard. She couldn't come to the competition because she had to work and didn't have enough money to travel anyway, but when she heard the news she was crying with joy. My mother and I had a good outlook after this. I was very happy at twelve years old. The competition gave me the feeling I was going to be someone special."

Other team members such as Nicole also outshined other competitors, but feeling special didn't last long, at least around Coach Ezra. Although the swimmers felt accomplished and happy being winners, this had a different meaning for the coach. Ezra's thinking was that when his swimmers felt special because of their success, this was incongruent to a good training strategy of improving them. Swimmers who were successful would not be treated with praise or looked upon by the rest of the team as great people. They were to be demeaned so they would try even harder to succeed. Ezra's sports psychology was much like that of a father who does not show love for his child while the child tries harder and harder to impress his or her father in hopes to receive love. Anna recalls: "His [Ezra's] psychology for our team was so bad. You would think he would be happy and treat you better. You would think you'd get some sort of benefit from winning or swimming well. For Ezra it was the opposite. He saw this as bad. He thought if you deny swimmers any privileges and degrade them in front of the other swimmers this would protect them from feeling special and push them to swim even better. The German swimmers weren't treated by their coach like this and they were good swimmers."

Everything seemed to go from a high to downhill with Ezra after their first major competition. Due to Ezra's psychological approach, Anna and Nicole didn't always feel like stars. Later Ezra's psychology became a serious problem. His degrading attitude started alienating them from the rest of the team. The less successful female swimmers started to see the more successful ones as people with problems who were not socially attractive. Teammates soon started distancing themselves from the best swimmers.

"He overly degraded us," Anna said, illustrating her point by grinding the tip of her thumb on the table. This is a gesture that means "to put someone in the dirt," or "to just plain humiliate someone." She continued, "I remember even before [the success at their first major meet] he called us names since we were nine years old, but it got really bad from around age twelve with our new success. He really started getting mean. He overly pushed and called names to the most successful swimmers. I think this was doing the opposite of what he wanted. I didn't feel this was helping me. How can you feel good about yourself when you believe you do what the coach asks and he still says things to you like 'fool,' 'idiot,' 'you're nothing,' 'you'll never be anyone'? We were just young girls, twelve years old and younger".

For a coach, a psychological strategy is always part of the overall training. Ezra's ideas of alienating the most successful team members were meant to protect them from the distractions that girls at this age may be experiencing. Ezra believed these distractions were not only arrogance and pride from swimming success, but also unwanted distractions from boys, gossip, and fashion that many girls overindulged themselves in. In hindsight one may see something wrong with his approach; for instance, why didn't he try other strategies as well? Could positive praise have helped? His strategy may nevertheless have had some potency of success since Anna and Nicole went on to become his most successful swimmers.

Nevertheless, if Ezra was seen as a kindly father figure early on, he was now showing signs of becoming a mean one with little care for his girls' feelings. Anna said, "Other girls on the team started disliking me, or at least acting like this when the coach was around, but he knew I was one of the best swimmers. Although he would degrade us, he wouldn't let any other team member do it. One time we just arrived for training in another city. We just got to the hotel and Ezra told us to gather around. I was arguing with another team member, Veronika. She said something rude to me that Ezra heard. He yelled at her saying, 'You are not worth the little toe on Anna's foot.' He said it so seriously like he really meant it. The whole team felt so bad for her. The funny thing is that we gathered around the coach because he was asking who wanted to share rooms with each other. Still, no one wanted to room with me because everyone sees how the coach treats me. It was like they don't want Ezra to think they like me. The girl that I ended up with was Eliska Roubichkova, my friend today. The reason being is that no one wanted to share a room with her, either. All this is because of the problems the trainer caused for us. He was making me an outcast of the group at the same time not letting anyone else say bad things about me. This was also true for the other good swimmers like Nicole. Whatever the coach said, it was like their father talking to them, because few girls had a real father living with them at home."

Soon after, Ezra went further with his sports psychology. He caused fear in the swimmers who wouldn't follow his rules. These rules went to an extreme that would be considered ridiculous to most people and coaches. They reached to all fathoms of the girls' lives. At such a young age, these girls didn't openly object too much even though they felt it was too excessive. If Ezra said something, the team just took it as normal without much thought, even though they disagreed, got angry, or became sad. Anna explained Ezra's rules and how the girls felt about their coach when they were twelve or so: "My coach made rules that we could not enter shops, look at displays in shop windows, wear makeup or jewelry, no talking to boys, no wearing fashionable clothes, we couldn't even go into cafés. These rules were not just when training and he was around, but for all times, even at home with your family. Even if you had some time off from training you still had to follow these rules. If the coach found out you were somewhere like a clothing shop, you would be punished", Anna.

Ezra had reasons for the rules he made. Many of the girls who followed these rules smile today at how absurd some of them were. One case of this absurdity was with their bathing suits. They didn't have anything but bottom underwear to use for swimsuits until the girls started to feel timid about swimming bare breasted in front of the coach and other boy teams. Knowing now what many of these girls would experience later in their careers, there is good reason to be suspicious about Ezra's delay in obtaining swimsuits for the female swimmers.

Anna recalls: "We had to wear our underwear bottoms as swimming trunks. In my city you couldn't buy [one-piece bathing suits] for girls' competitions, but our coach surely could have gotten them. We didn't care so much about swimming bare breasted when we were children, but at twelve, some of us already were developing breasts. We started asking about getting real swimsuits, but the coach's reasons were that they'll decrease our speed. The most ridiculous thing he said was that wearing a bathing suit would make us feel like grown ups and cause us to think about other things. Instead of buying them, the coach agreed later that our parents could sew a piece of material connecting both sides from our hips of our underwear to the sides of a bra. They looked ridiculous but they worked for the time being." Swimmers would be punished just for complaining too much about such conditions as these.

Punishment took the form of hard training and exercise such as pushups, pull-ups, running, and laps in the pool. The coach made this worse by verbally abusing the girls when they were in trouble. The girls really started to fear him and didn't like him being around. It wasn't because he would hit them yet, but how he would treat and talk to them. Anna explains a funny story but it illustrates the fear that the coach started causing some girls. "We were in our home city. I think we were about twelve or thirteen. It was winter, and there was a lot of snow on the ground. We just left the swimming pool on our way somewhere, I can't really remember. We left before the coach, so we thought we were far ahead of him. Another teammate named Tanya and I stopped at a little kiosk to look at some pencils, gum, and other little things. Then we saw the coach coming up. Tanya thought she wasn't seen yet, so she ran behind the kiosk and dug a hole in the snow and tried to burry herself. She just didn't want to get yelled at or made to feel stupid anymore. I stood there because I knew the coach already saw both of us. He told me to come with him and we went behind the kiosk and saw part of Tanya sticking out of the snow. He jokingly asked what she was doing under all that snow. Tanya came out and we both stood there knowing we were going to get punished. He said we have to do many laps to-morrow, butterfly style. He had been treating us like this for too long now and I was getting angry about it. I was beginning to be stubborn and was tired of his behavior. I always felt I wasn't afraid of the coach like most others were. Tanya accept-ed her punishment but I said, 'I'm not doing it, because we were only looking at little things that I thought were meaningless.' When I said, 'I'm not going to do laps for this,' he looked at me and said, 'What? You're not going to do what I say?' He told me to go home and I'm not on the team anymore. Just for that?! I got angry and took the bus home. I told my mother everything and she was disappointed that I left the team. I said I didn't want to go back, but she tried to encourage me. I told her what reasons we would be punished for and the worst was just showing up one minute late. The public transport in this country is so bad. The buses come whenever they come. You could wait 2 minutes or 30 minutes and if they don't come because of an accident nobody comes to tell all the people at the stops. There is no set schedule, and who had cars at that time. After I told my mother the coach's ridiculous rules and how we get punished for them she said, 'Well, if you don't want to go back then you don't have to.' I was happy that I stood up to him and happy that my mother supported my decision, but I was unhappy that I wasn't swimming. I'm sure that Ezra was expecting me to show up for training the next morning. I didn't. Then later that night he came over to my home. He was so nice to my mother and me. He apologized and asked if I would come back to the team the next morning. I really wanted to keep swimming but I knew even at that time he would still treat us the same way, but I sucked it up and went back."

Coach Ezra's apologizing became a recurring theme. His behavior didn't change. In fact, Ezra's behavior started to become worse and worse. He was correctly suspected by the team of drinking too much at times, which may have exacerbated the existing problems of his treatment of team members. Ezra's abusive behavior coupled with his use of alcohol as a self-remedy likely only increased the probability of more problems. But what exactly were his problems? Was he just under stress because of the excitement that he was coaching swimmers who could be future world-class or Olympic competitors and didn't want to relax a psychological strategy he thought was working? Was he unhappy with something but thought it necessary to continue treating swimmers this way although it made the team members unhappy? Or, was Ezra suffering from other things psychological, such as thoughts and temptations that would not or should not be acceptable to society? I as well as former members of his team believe all of the above. All of these factors led him to turn even more to the bottle. His alcoholism may have promoted a cycle of escalating abuse as well as a temptation to use different, harsher forms of abuse. Later events would very much seem to support these claims.

5

The Passing of Grandma and
a Nation in Decay (1990)

It wasn't long after Aunt Lydie moved in with the couple that was supposed to care for her in exchange for her pension when a telegram arrived. It was from an old-folks' home. Anna and her mother had neither heard from nor visited Aunt Lydie in the last month. The telegram was only a couple of sentences long. Anna read it to her mother, who was home at the time. It said that Lydie had died. There wasn't any further information; nothing. They were confused. Why had she been at an old-folks' home? She should have been living with friends. Mariana quickly went to the old-folks' home that day, but was upset and disappointed by the response she received from the staff. They said Lydie did die, but that they didn't know when or even where she was buried. Unbelievable! The staff even got upset after Mariana demanded more information about the cause of death and the location of the body. Pleading became futile and she left empty handed, with no more information than what was in the telegram sent to them earlier in the day.

Anna recalls: "This was the saddest thing in my life. My Great-Aunt Lydie who I always felt was my grandmother died and there was no explanation of why. The staff at the old-folks' home didn't even care and got upset when my mother was asking them where she was buried. What kind of country is this when you have people like this in it? You are just left crying for weeks, wondering what happened. She was healthy just a month ago, walking and talking just like anyone else. She never had a diagnosis for any problem or disease. Our family thinks that she was deliberately left to die after something like a sudden heart attack and someone stole the things she had. She went to the couple's house with all her belongings, and she had some nice things as well as money, more than most older people. She saved her money and always gave me some for ice cream and sweets when my mother had none. What makes us think she was left to die is that none of her belongings were given back to us from the couple or the old folk's home. She had nice things like knitted wool blankets and sweaters she made herself. She even had a whole box of things like pictures, books and jewelry that she said would be mine when she went to heaven. The staff said they didn't know about any such belongings and that Lydie just lived there and died there. This sounds cruel, but this is exactly how these people behaved, like they didn't care. Later we found out that her so-called friends who took her in were the ones who put her in the old folk's home. They just wanted her pension money and put her in the home after a couple months of taking care of her. Maybe they were the ones who took her things and brought her to the home with nothing. We just don't know exactly what happened nor anyone cares to tell us, and the police at that time wouldn't even care if we told them."

The behavior of her grandmother's so-called friends and the staff at this Soviet-style old folk's home was nothing uncommon. I think here, at the end of this chapter, a little background history of Eastern Europe's Communist era is necessary for those who have not studied or did not experience it. This will help illustrate why such attitudes existed at the time and why they still very much exist today. At the same time it will illustrate the reasons behind the attitudes and behaviors of most workers, Soviet citizens, and especially the characters of our story.

From its inception, The Soviet Union had gone through many disasters caused by human error that made life unnecessarily harder. From Lenin to Stalin through the final years of the Soviet Union, policies were made by those who had loyalty to the government instead of by those who had merit and who could get the job done correctly. Collectivization and *kolkhozes* (state-owned farms based on Marxist ideology that were meant to improve efficiency but failed in practice) were forced on its peasants and farmers. The Soviet government tried to improve industrialization by employing more people without focusing on technology. Too many great minds fled or were oppressed because their thinking was not politically correct for the government. The distribution of equal services to every citizen taxed the economy so much that everyone ended up being poor. Those citizens who could work harder than most of the others would not, because their extra labor would be wasted on those who didn't work as hard. Centralization in faraway Moscow, where the Soviet Union was controlled, kept the policy makers out of touch with those in other Soviet countries and regions. These were the major causes for the famous bread lines that were seen on Western T.V.

The Soviet Union had vast amounts of land that was useful for more than just farming. It had huge oil reserves, gold deposits, huge aluminum mines, and a population that was willing to learn and work. Russia alone is a country bigger than the United States with fewer people to feed but more land in which to feed them. There is no excuse for the downfall of the Soviet Union other than utter human mismanagement based on a stubborn policy to prove to the world that Marxist policies are better than the rest. The Soviet and especially the Ukrainian people suffered for this. Too many people in these countries were poor, and they were working for much less than what they deserved. They couldn't travel outside the Soviet Union or buy goods that could lessen the burdens of life. Technology from the space and military industry was not given to public industries to improve housing, household goods, city infrastructure, or, most importantly, to build an information technology industry in which computers could have greatly reduced the country's labor burden. There was little incentive to work, try harder, or be happy. The USSR collapsed.

State workers still make up a large percentage of the workforce. They are paid extremely low wages. Anna's mother worked in a middle school and made the equivalent of only $58 a month when I visited them in 2004. Doctors who made regular house calls only made about $85 a month at this time, and workers at the post office made about $35 a month. Consider that at the same time, the cost of a cheap apartment and utilities were around $100 to $150 a month. Only a few privately operated businesses can pay their employees decent wages to make living comfortable.

At the time when Anna's Great-Aunt Lydie died in 1990, everyone in her country was a state worker no matter what his or her profession. Everybody was getting paid low wages and the shelves at the market had little food, sometimes none at all. The conditions were not improving and the country was about to find itself in political turmoil with the sudden change to a more democratic government in the late eighties and early nineties. The Soviet attitude quickly became "take all you can for yourself now because it might not be there tomorrow." From that time, many had the attitude to steal everything they could grab and sell anything to make a dollar. Many former Soviet citizens are like that today, not because their job conditions are sometimes hideous, but rather because they don't get paid enough to feel that an honest job is worth doing. These citizens often have attitudes that are rude, unhelpful, and unmotivated. On top of this, most still believe like they did under Communism - anyone in a higher position than himself or herself can do what he or she wants to, so it is no use to fight or even question them, as is the case in military hierarchies. All of the conditions mentioned above are burdensome for the whole population of the former Soviet countries and cause inefficiency, error, mismanagement, and even worse, stealing, abuse, exploitation, and murder. One can only wonder why Anna's grandmother disappeared in a way that was not much different than her real grandfather did during World War Two.

6

Building Success, Going International, A Nation in Change, and Serious Rumors (1990-1992)

After the death of Aunt Lydie, Anna focused on what she had. "I had friends from the team that were doing the same things I was, training. There were even some relatives of mine that lived in my city and, of course, my mother. This is what helped me after Grandma died. I felt my mother and swimming were the only positive things in my life when I was thirteen. With dedication to swimming I could shut out all of life's other problems," Anna said.

Her difficulties were not enough to deter her from swimming. At the age of thirteen, she and her teammates were preparing for major, nationally recognized meets. At this time she was appointed her swimming style, which she would concentrate on for the rest of her career. She recalls: "I was good in all other styles except for the butterfly. Our team didn't have a female member at this time that was training for the breast stroke competitions, so my coach picked me. I really didn't understand because I was very good at freestyle. My freestyle times were the best on the team, slightly faster than Nicole's, whose style was always the freestyle."

They were entering their first international meets with competitors from within and outside of the Soviet Union. One was the International Meet in Bulgaria. Here Anna made friends with the German girls' team. She says: "The Germans noticed what bad condition our swimsuits were in, with many stitchings and little holes. Ezra only gave us one swimsuit for training and competition which we used for so long now. We constantly had to sew them up. We were afraid while competing in front of people they would tear open. The German girls gave some of us one of their own suits since they all had a couple. That was the first real good swimsuits some of us got." Regardless of the condition of their swimsuits, some of Ezra's swimmers fared very well. Anna herself won first place in two breast stroke competitions. Two weeks later in another meet of all the nation's top swimmers, Anna won first place and another second place. Nicole also won a couple of first places at these meets. Because of their excellent performances, they were pushed into a more prestigious light among fellow Soviet swimmers.

"We were excited that we were becoming good, and other swimmers started to know who we were. Swimmers started coming to competitions and knowing that you are the favorite. It was really fun and exciting," Anna.

This year (1990) some members of Ezra's team were good enough to join the Junior National Swim Team, and naturally Nicole and Anna were among them. Anna felt great about this. This would not just mean a step up in competition and a chance for higher glory, but it would also mean that she would have the chance to travel more of the world, which most Soviet citizens were not allowed to do.

Ezra and his swimmers were getting recognition and he was surely delighted. His own dedication to the sport he loved had paid off. His newly budding success may have caused great joy, but it also instilled in him an even harder drive for further success. The hard training increased, as did the mental stress. As members of the Junior

National Swim Team, they would now be representing at international meets one of the most powerful nations on earth, The Soviet Union. But this would not last long. In just over a year they would have their first international competition experience outside of the USSR, not as Soviet swimmers, but as swimmers of their own country.

A Nation in Change

The last Soviet leader, Mikhail Gorbachev, implemented hard-fought democratic reforms resulting in the first-ever democratic presidential elections in June of 1991. Boris Yeltsin was elected President in the first elections, and in December, Russia, The Ukraine and Belarus abolished the USSR and formed the CIS. Gorbachev, as head of the Communist Party, later that month announced that the USSR had ceased to exist.

The Cold War had practically ended and the victory was for all countries under Soviet central rule; Russia, Czechoslovakia, Bulgaria, Romania, Latvia, Lithuania, Estonia, Kazakhstan, Poland, Hungary and others. The transition for these now or soon-to-be independent countries was not a smooth one. Because of years of bureaucratic

Communist governing, there weren't many ideas in these nations of how a free market, privatization, or democratic government should work, but these problems little affected Ezra's swimmers.

Serious Rumors

Nicole and Anna had already placed among the Soviet's best swimmers at both the International meet in Bulgaria and the meet between the nation's top swimmers. The beginning of the nineties appeared to start out great for both of them although the Soviet Union was collapsing and their country, although with renewed independence, was in turmoil.

There was no doubt at this point that both girls had made it to the world-class level. Though there was triumph, there was also the beginning of the hint of tragedy. Nineteen ninety-one began the time of serious rumors. They mainly consisted of stories about Coach Ezra spending an unusual amount of time late at night with one of his top swimmers, Nicole. The rumors were not hard to believe, since Ezra and Nicole began staying in the same room when traveling during 1990 when she was only thirteen. When staying at KA-14, she was seen numerous times by other swimmers and staff coming back to her room late at night and in the early morning from where the coach slept. They even started showing up in the mornings together for training.

Anna tells: "Everyone on the team, including Ezra's boys' team, started talking about this. Nicole was seen so many times coming back from the coach's room late at night and early in the morning. What is she doing there at that time of night? We were young and thought it funny and made jokes about it. We didn't really know at that time what exactly was going on, but we all thought he was having sex with her."

Rumors are only rumors until those involved admit to them, and Nicole never divulged a thing when her fellow swimmers subtly joked with her about it. She went about her training and competing just like she did before these rumors began circulating, as did the rest of the team. There was no need to ponder these rumors or even the nations' problems with so many competitions coming up.

(1992)

Though Yeltsin and Gorbachev may have been seen as superstars to the rest of the world and many Soviet people, they had no concrete, organized plan ready to put in place once Communism ended. Because of this, mass disorganization, confusion, and crime reigned for the next few years in many former Soviet countries. The ruble and other former Soviet currencies plummeted in value on January 2, 1992, and in April the once great nation of Russia received a $24 billion aid package from other Western nations that was to be used to help build infrastructure and repair the economy.

Fourteen-year-old Anna and Nicole's country suffered greatly during this time as they entered into their 1992 swimming season. Their country was poor, confused, and in a state of chaos; but despite all of this, there was optimism for the future. Their country's optimism came not only from those of the older generation who pushed to change things for the better during the final days of Communism, but most of all it radiated from its future; its young people.

This was also the year of Barcelona, the 1992 Olympic Games. Anna's and Nicole's performances were crucial. They had two events before they would go on to the national championships in the capital. They would also have to perform well and not injure themselves to be able to make the Olympic Games. The two events before the national championships were the national finals and the world junior championship. The national finals was a gathering in the capital of the nation's junior swimmers without the presence of swimmers from the national team. In this event Nicole and Anna came out in the top spots.

The second meet was the world junior championships in Stockholm, Sweden. This had a whole different meaning for the girls. Nicole and Anna would get their first experience outside of the former Soviet states while representing their nation. Traveling was one of the most enjoyable things about being on the team. There would be members from all over the world. The pressure and excitement built. As in most sports, the junior team was the next step to the national team, and this was the dream for all of Ezra's team members. The national team would ultimately be the one to represent their country in the Olympics and world championships.

Stockholm was also the chance to meet swimmers from other countries, to talk with them, to know their opinions, and to make friends. The girls on the team really enjoyed this but there was still the old air of mistrust. The team was lectured by Ezra before traveling internationally not to talk with swimmers of other countries—some feelings of the Cold War still remained for some, but not so much for the young swimmers. They weren't thinking about any war, no matter how cold it was. They just wanted to meet new people, and the curiosity was too great for some, especially Anna, who many times was the first team member to try to make friends. She remembers: "I met nice girls from Canada, Slovakia, and Austria. It was nice to see how friendly we all were with one another. It was fun to talk with them and now, since we could travel more, we would be sure to tell each other 'hey, I'll see you at the next competition,' and we usually would end up seeing each other and go out after meets."

At Stockholm, Ezra's team had new social and cultural experiences while showing friendly faces to the world and coming away with winning results. In the breast stroke, Anna won two first places and one second place while Nicole took two first places in the freestyle competitions. These girls were building a great reputation with their victories, and their families were elated. Their swim times were improving. They were some of the top swimmers in their country at the young age of fourteen. At this point the girls' succeeding to the next step, the national team, was a forgone conclusion. With their results from Stockholm, they had the confidence and times to compete against national team members in the national championships. The top swimmers from this competition would go on to the Olympic Games held in Barcelona that year, just as long as they qualified under two rules: they must have the best time in their event at the national champion-ship, and that time must be as good as or better than the Olympic standard times for eligibility.

At the national championships, Nicole came on top, but Anna lost to an older national team member by a few one-hundredths of a second. Because of this, Nicole would be going to Barcelona while Anna stayed home. But, the results allowed both girls to be on the national team, and they would now be able to represent their country in every major world swimming competition. The honor was extraordinary, but it was already expected by Anna, who described her and Nicole's excitement as modest.

7

The Olympics, Drinking, and the Physical Abuse Begins

As for Ezra's behavior during the successful events leading up to the 1992 Olympics, he was described as worse with his strict rules and mental mistreatment. His swimmers loathed him. The girls dreaded the degradation and punishment, which they were forced to go through constantly. Although his physical training was never a problem, when it came to fundamentals, the girls liked it more when he wasn't around. Whatever the case, he still was pushing some of them on to victory, even though his methods were not making him any friends. There was another factor starting to evolve that affected his training as well: alcohol. His swimmers noticed that he had started drinking much more.

It should be noted that drinking is very common in some cultures. This is the case in Anna's country. There, it's not unusual to see people drinking during working hours or on their lunch breaks, whether they are businessmen or government workers. Drinking is such a part of the culture there that today it is one of the leading causes of death among men. Alcohol, together with a stressful lifestyle, is such a burden on males that their average life expectancy has been lingering well below that of American males. Fortunately, the women are much different and are not known for their drinking like their male counterparts. This gives them a life expectancy very similar to the female European average. With this in mind, it is easy to see why it was not surprising to the swimmers or their parents that Ezra drank alot. It's just part of the culture.

Ezra, like many other coaches, would celebrate his victories with some alcohol. He was already well known by his swimmers for this type of celebrating. Anna says: "Our coach would usually get together after competitions with the assistant coaches and coaches of other teams and drink. This was quite normal and we didn't think this strange at all, but we did notice he was drinking a lot more on regular occasions. He came [around 1991] a few times to training drunk in the morning. This was a problem that was small but started to become bigger and bigger. He just started drinking more and more. He would always be drunk when we traveled." One plane ride home illustrates an episode of Ezra's behavior that caused more than just embarrassment for his team.

Some time after the '92 Olympics, Ezra and some of his team members were returning from a competition on an international flight. He and a coach from another team had been drinking before they got on the plane. Once on the plane, they kept drinking, becoming louder, and singing songs. It was already annoying for the people on the plane, and it got worse when both coaches found under their seats life preservers used in case of a crash in water. They were not inflated and the coaches only had to pull their cords for them to quickly and automatically fill with air, and this is just what they did. They began to blow their coach's whistles while dancing in the isles. This of course became too much, and the flight stewardess reprimanded them and an argument ensued. The coaches did get back in their seats, but they had caused a great embarrassment to the national team and national sports committee. This incident made its way into some newspapers with the final result of Ezra being banned for two years by the national sports committee from traveling by plane. This meant he would miss some international events. Drinking wasn't the only problem people noticed.

Anna and Nicole were just a pair from the team who proved good enough to compete in major events. They would travel extensively together while competing. Nicole and Anna roomed with each other most of this time on domestic and international trips. Anna became aware of incidents between the coach and Nicole in '91.

Anna remembers: "Nicole and I were staying together when we were training in the capital. It was later in the evening when we finished training. I was sitting in my room reading when Nicole came in crying, covering her face. She went straight to her bed next to mine and lay with her face in the pillow. She just came from Ezra's room and she was cursing his name. I really felt that I didn't want to get involved and Nicole just kept crying. I didn't ask her about anything but I saw she got beaten. She didn't tell me anything. She just cried. Although I felt uncomfortable, I went on just reading."

This wasn't the only time Anna saw her friend in such a condition after coming from Ezra's room. From this point on it started happening several times per year, and never during this time did Nicole tell Anna exactly what was going on.

Everyone kept on swimming and the rumors kept building. The boys' team noticed all this as well, and was gossiping about the rumors with us. Nicole was of course left out of this, and would not even make comments when people would make a joke to her in an attempt to divulge some information about her having sex or getting beaten by Ezra.

Anna felt the right thing to do was to ignore the problems Nicole was going through. They were just thirteen at the time and the need to deal with such problems was something not expected from children their age. "Nicole never asked for any sort of help so I felt like I should not get involved," Anna said about the situation. She was not being directly affected, so to her, the problems others might have been experiencing were just that, problems of others. This all would soon change for her.

As for Nicole, she would be turning fourteen in May, just before the Olympics. She may have come into contact with some serious problems she thought could never be possible, but she was still swimming, and she would still be competing in the Olympics.

Barcelona was Nicole's debut Olympics. It was her first time in Spain, and she found things there to be quite in contrast with the lifestyles of her country. The shelves were full for everyone, not just for the athletes and government officials, as was the situation in her country. She was always with Ezra, and he was drunk most of the time. They had little chance to really explore, as their government funding budget did not allow them to leave the local area, and left them with little money of their own to do anything. Nicole was only there for one reason, however— to fulfill the dream to be known as an Olympian. She hoped for the best, but at a young age she was happy when she placed seventh in her event.

Ironically enough, Anna was swimming at a minor competition in her country during the Olympics. This time, with her mother in the stands, she broke the country's one hundred meter breast stroke record with a time better than the swimmer who had beaten her at the national championships to make the Olympic team. As well, Anna's time was even better than her team-mate had in the Olympics.

As for Ezra, his constant drinking in Barcelona was the first sign of what would be his usual behavior from now on. It developed into a serious concern not just for the girls, but for the whole team. Years later some of Ezra's swimmers told me they didn't know exactly when the serious drinking started, but that it was probably before '92. His behavior started to deteriorate and he began missing training for days at a time. The behavior did not just progress to an increase in his already degrading sports psychology; it progressed to abuse in much more serious forms. Anna had already seen Nicole abused at the hands of her coach earlier this year, and she would soon experience the abuse herself.

Repulsed by what the girls saw going on around them, especially when compared with their new experiences in other Western countries, they naturally started dreaming of things that could be. They felt helpless to make the situation better in their own country. The problems they were dealing with did not come only from their coach, but also from the society they came from in general. It was on the edge of collapse. The

optimism that appeared in former Soviet countries after the fall of communism was waning.
The economy and unemployment worsened as
the majority of the nation became poorer. Crime
was rising, and those affected by it had almost no
legal avenues for justice. Though they were being
affected personally in the situation with Ezra, the
lack of an effective justice system left Nicole and
Anna feeling powerless to change anything.

8

Dreaming of a Better Life (1993)

With Ezra's growing success he started attracting better swimmers from different parts of the country trying to build an even better team. It was now 1993. Swimming was Nicole and Anna's life. All the things that other girls their age were doing, they were not, nor would they be doing them anytime soon. Boys were off-limits, going to the ever-popular discos in Europe was off-limits, shopping in stores was off-limits, jewelry was off-limits; even dressing up and going to cafés was not allowed. It may come into question whether or not taking these extreme measures to isolate the team was a reasonable way to improve results. Whatever the case, their results were improving. The girls had no choice but to make such sacrifices to be on the team. They made the national team the year before, an enormous accomplishment in itself. They made it to every major world swimming event. Nicole even went to the '96 Olympics, and Anna had her eye firmly on the next one.

Big meets now happened about twice per year with more of the usual, smaller meets inside the country. The girls wanted to keep their rankings up and their places high so that they could keep taking part in the big meets such as the national, European, and world championships, and of course the Olympics. Taking part in these events was not the whole point. Aside from the heightened self-esteem and the glory of winning, the real fun was always going to countries and cities they'd never been to before.

The common people of Anna's country felt that Western nations were highly developed, and their citizens lived far better lives than they did. Seeing their nation in decay trying to pick up the pieces from an ill-planned governmental transition, along with having to put up with a deviant coach, made these girls yearn for a life in the West.

Though travel restrictions were lifted a bit after the latest elections, it was still extremely hard to take a trip out of the country due to cost. Most people didn't even have cars, and if they did it probably wasn't in any condition to make trips farther than a family cottage outside the city.

The black market developed at an astonishing pace. There one could buy almost anything, from toilet paper to military weapons straight from the military. Everyone was involved to some extent in this makeshift system of supply and demand. Violence between groups trying to control a small section of kiosks to those killing industry bosses in order to corner a market was rising at a shocking rate. In 1994 alone over two hundred industrial and banking bosses were gunned down. With statistics like this it was no wonder that every facet of criminality was on the rise. The police and judicial system had a very weak grasp of order. Everyone in a high position was most likely in someone else's pocket, doing favor after favor for a favor in return. The strong and ruthless were coming out on top, and morality was hitting rock bottom. Business ethics were meaningless which scared away foreign investors.

State coffers were nearly empty, as taxes were hard to collect. The elderly whose state benefits were drastically cut suffered the most. Those who didn't have the strength to work begged. Those who could work were on the sidewalk sell-ing anything they could from behind a table or on a blanket. The most fortunate of the elderly, as well as some of the younger citizens, had cottages where they grew fruits and vegetables. This provided them with produce to sell as well as something to eat. People were going hungry, and the infamous Russian breadlines that Americans saw on television were just as common in Anna's country. For the many who owned cottages, this is what kept them from being completely penniless and malnourished. The luckiest citizens had some sort of farm where they had abundant meat, poultry, and milk products, but the availability of these goods to the average person was rare during the mid-nineties. It was becoming chaotic and unstable, and it was no place for parents to raise children.

This does a lot for someone when they witness it, let alone go through it. Anna and Nicole were good swimmers whom the state took care of so that they could compete. They had the food they needed to stay in peak performance, far more than most had. Many swimmers like Anna gave their families what they were able to bring home from training.

It is evident that it was extra special to be on a sports team during these times. National team members like Anna and Nicole found it very disastrous to see their country barren of food and the basic necessities, especially while traveling to Western countries where almost no one worries about going to sleep hungry. In other countries the swimmers saw what was possible for their country, which was currently stricken with crime and poverty. Necessities and stability could be obtained in other countries, along with the pleasures and luxuries they created. At the time, these girls never thought they would really search for a life outside their country, but they started to dream about this. Why? They simply wanted a better quality of life. Anna recalls: "I would travel to other countries like England, France, and Italy and the people there had the chance to buy anything they wanted. There were always full shelves at even the littlest grocery store. They had fruits and vegetables I'd never seen before. No one was complaining about the lack of work and families were going on vacation together weeks at a time in the summer. If the common person lived like this, I'm sure national sport stars were probably a little better off. The only thing I missed from my country while traveling was my mother and friends. Besides that, I would have stayed forever in Western Europe somewhere if I could."

9

Focus on Abuse

For the swimmers the team was at one point a safe haven that kept them away from the rest of society's problems, but this safety seriously waned around 1993. Ezra's physical abuse was soon to spread to other swimmers. Coupled with his alcoholism, there began a serious lack of team leadership.

Anna tells: "Ezra began getting fatter in '92, and then he got a really big stomach around '94. He became seriously unhealthy, and we knew why since we always saw him drunk from around '93. I think ever since 1994 he showed up to training in the morning drunk." Years later, Nicole told me that Ezra's parents also had serious problems with alcoholism that most likely had a bad influence on him. Not only was Ezra's body becoming unhealthy, but his inappropriate behaviors were intensifying.

A few incidents that would surely not be tolerated by any American professional sports organization exemplify the effects his alcoholism had on his career. A comical but embarrassing incident happened at the national sporting complex in the capital. Early in the morning, Ezra's team was waiting for him in front of the complex. By this time, his being late was common. "Then another coach showed up with his team. He started joking with us, saying, 'when are you guys going to join your coach for some singing.' This coach explained that on his way here, just down the road other swimmers and coaches were passing by Ezra drunk sitting with a bottle under a tree singing. This coach told us we should go and get him because he's not coming if we don't. It was embarrassing because people started to know who the coach was not for his coaching but more for his drunken behavior. Some of us had to go down the road to ask our coach how we had to train today. He gave them instructions and we swam without him," Anna.

It became all too common for Ezra not to show up to training sessions in the team's home city at all for the whole day, a few days, and sometimes a whole week. Moreover, anytime the team trained outside their home city they couldn't get into the training facility without a coach. More often than not, the team had to wait outside of a training center because Ezra showed up late or not at all. The hypocrisy, of course, is that his swimmers would be punished for showing up even one minute late.

Anna recalls: "There are so many times where he didn't show up for practice and we were all waiting outside the swimming pool. Then a pool worker would come out and tell us he called and left a note at the front desk with the receptionist. The note was what training we had to do for the day. We would all be so happy when he didn't come for training. We started feeling like this around 1993. We didn't like him as a coach and how he treated us. We could see he wouldn't change and his drinking was very unattractive. The worst thing about him not coming to practice is that sometimes we had big competitions coming up. Some swimmers need to train more and some need to relax. Everyone is different and they need to train certain ways the last few weeks before a meet. The notes he left were so general and you could imagine how some of us wouldn't push ourselves when he wasn't around.

Many of us were determined and wanted to win so we still trained hard, but you still need a coach for directions and details. That's why you have a coach. All year you train for something big and your coach doesn't show up for training before the competition. This was a serious problem. I felt like he was ruining us and our chances to win. I know we would have done a little better in many more competitions if so many times he didn't miss so many days."

Not only did Ezra drink, but he also broke his own rules about letting his swimmers drink. At the ages of fifteen and sixteen, his swimmers who were training to be world class athletes had little interest in alcohol, but they thought the last person to tempt them would be their coach.

Anna says: "We were going on some sporting trip by train and Ezra called me to his room. We talked about little things for a minute, then he offered me a shot of vodka. I started thinking he was joking. I kind of laughed and said no. He didn't say anything and started drinking, so I just got up and left. You know, you can't drink or do things that a normal girl wants to do like go to discos and café's because of the coach's rules and training, then that same coach tries to get you to drink vodka with him, even though we're going to train for a big international meet. And so many times he was drunk yelling and hitting some of us for little things. I didn't want to be around that. I didn't think till maybe a year later that he may have been offering me alcohol for other reasons."

Offering alcohol to a fifteen- year-old is hardly a crime in any country, but this was the least serious of Anna's accusations toward her coach. At fifteen, Anna had two incidents that completely shocked her.

In '93 the girls were training for the European sprint championships and the world long course championships. Anna remembers: "Our team went for a few days to the capital and trained at the national sports complex. We were preparing for upcoming competitions. One time after training I was told by an assistant coach to come with him. Ezra, our coach, wanted to see me in his room. We walked in. He was sitting down and, like usual, he was drunk. He did not say a word to me. He got up, walked towards me, and hit me really hard with the palm of his hand. He hit me right below my eye and I flew back. I started crying and had no idea why he was doing this. Maybe I swam bad or something. I couldn't believe it. I was shocked. He didn't say anything and I ran to my room crying."

The next day, the assistant coach that witnessed it all came to my room and saw that my eye was blue. He was apologizing for Ezra. He said that Ezra was drunk and didn't know what he was doing. I'm sure he told Ezra about my eye turning blue because he came soon after the assistant coach left. He saw my eye and apologized, saying he didn't know why he did it. He again talked nice and innocent so I wouldn't leave the team or tell someone like my mother. If my mother knew she would force me to leave the team."

Anna didn't tell her mother, but she knew there was no excuse for Ezra to hit her in the eye. Why would someone deserve to get hit in this situation? She was a fifteen-year-old girl with a drunken coach. She now started realizing what Nicole was going through on the many times she had come back to their room crying.

This was not the only time he laid his hand across the face of Anna. Later she had a similar experience when they were at the pool at KA-14.

Anna recalls: "I was fifteen or sixteen, I think. It wasn't long after he hit me in the national sports complex. My coach called me into his room again. It was just like before, but this time Nicole was already there in his room. She stood off to the side of him, and I could see she was scared already and a little battered. I could see Ezra was drunk. He closed the door behind me and locked it. I got scared and started crying. He again said nothing and then started hitting Nicole. He then quickly turned to me and hit me in the face. Again, I didn't know the reason for it at all. He doesn't say really anything and just starts hitting you." This time Anna ran out of the room and away from KA-14. She ran all the way to her home on Afinska Street swearing she wouldn't return.

Ezra was now at the point of hitting his swimmers in front of the rest of the team, including his assistant coaches. Not only were they seeing the abuse, but other teams were also getting a glimpse of it. Around this time, Ezra got upset with Nicole and, in front of other swimmers and coaches at the national sports complex, shoved her flat on her back at poolside. Anna was doing laps in the pool at the time and didn't know what had happened until training was done. "Other girls from the team came to my room and asked if I saw what happened. I didn't. They said how he shoved her and she fell right on her back in front of the other teams. That is how things were. It happened when I was right there but I couldn't tell as everyone was the same when I started my laps than when I finished. No one wants to get involved. People are obviously troubled that something happens but just act like they don't notice. We felt bad for Nicole, but what could you do. There was no one you could complain to about your coach."

Anna, more stubborn than the rest, had the courage to speak up one day after witnessing Nicole getting beaten again. Months later, the team was once more training in the capital at the national sports complex, and again both Nicole and Anna found themselves at night after training with Ezra in his room. Ezra started yelling at both the girls over training. Again he got upset enough and started beating Nicole. Anna explained, "I was so scared when he started beating her. He was smacking her in the head and face and I just closed my eyes. I was hoping he wasn't going to start hitting me. Luckily he didn't. He stopped and started yelling but things calmed down. A few minutes later when he was not so hostile I had enough strength to tell him that if he ever hits me again I will leave the team. I said it clear enough so he really believed I was serious. He just gave me a mean look but I saw he believed what I said." After Anna told the coach these things, she was lucky enough even after some hostile moments not to be hit by him again. She believed the reason was that Ezra probably felt his influence was waning a bit as the girls were getting older. Maybe if the other girls who were being abused would have spoken up like Anna, their abuse would have ceased.

As an American I know what would happen if an American coach would hit one of his teen-age swimmers. There would be much to answer for, as well as fines, loss of jobs, court hearings and parents pushing for the maximum punishment for the offender. But this wasn't the case in Anna's country. Americans have heard the stories of how some Soviet coaches beat their players. We know this is neither necessary nor right. Would it have helped if others would have had enough courage to at least tell Ezra to stop like Anna did? Would the physical abuse have stopped if someone had made those above Ezra aware of it, or would they have cared? In fact, who was above Ezra; the Olympic Committee?

He was an Olympic coach coaching an Olympic team. Did the Olympic Committee know of or at least hear of anything going on? For that matter, do they have any structure of responsibility in place in case such matters arise?

With this story as an example, I don't see a system to deal with such things besides the police, who only take notice if someone higher up instructs them to do so. The police are underpaid and overworked. In Anna's country during the time that these events took place, there were no major influential organizations that dealt with the abuse of children in order to protect them, and there still are not any today. Anyone under Soviet rule—especially Eastern Europeans—had the attitude that if injustice is done to you by anyone in a higher position, it is pointless to fight it. They had a very defeatist attitude towards life: if you are an underdog you will stay that way. Again you must look at the Soviet governmental and social system which developed from a military-type chain of command. Nobody in this system went over the head of the boss, and if the boss was doing someone harm, he or she couldn't do much about it.

As I explained, these attitudes still very much exist today and one can see why Nicole and Anna, even though they were abused, thought it was pointless to make accusations against their coach. For them, the only option was to leave the team and get away from Ezra.

10

Sexual Abuse No Longer Rumors

The 1994 swimming season was packed with all sorts of international meets in Germany, Austria, Italy, and even Argentina. Saint Petersburg, Russia would also be hosting this year's Goodwill Games. This year was also filled with some big surprises. At one meet alone, Nicole broke her country's 100 meter freestyle record, and Nicole and Anna again broke the old record for the four women 4×100 meter combination. With national records their media attention grew, but not all of the attention was good. At the Goodwill Games, right after the event, the swimmers were tested for drug use. Brometine was found in Nicole's system. Brometine was not a banned substance, but it was still a performance enhancer that was also used to mask steroids in the body. Due to this, she was disqualified. Of course Ezra refuted any wrongdoing or involvement, but a few years later he would be in the center of another much larger doping scandal.

Besides the small stain that was solely placed on Nicole, the girls never thought they'd do so well when they started at the age of seven. They began to get more recognition, and the attention filled them with joy. They felt good. They were at their peak. They broke records held by their country's best swimmers from the past. In view of the sports media, it couldn't get much better than this, but out of view, the abuse got worse. There were other surprises in store this year. This year would be very revealing for Anna regarding the abuse Nicole was going through.

They were at the Latin America's Cup held in Buenos Aires, Argentina. The girls had a blast seeing a country so far away in another hemisphere. Besides the beautiful tourist beaches and the warm, humid weather, they were much more struck by the poverty and the necessity of having an escort every time they left the hotel so as not to get victimized.

This meet was an especially fruitful one for Anna. She didn't just come home with four first places and two second places; she was also the female Absolute Champion of the meet, meaning she was rated the best overall female swimmer.

On the plane home from Argentina, the girls were happy to be relaxing from a long, successful meet, especially Anna, who suffered from a rough case of strep throat. There were only three girls from Ezra's team who went to this meet: Nicole, Anna, and another by the name of Luska. They all sat together in a row of three seats. Nicole was sitting in the middle. The only other team-mate accompanying the girls was an assistant coach who was sitting a few seats back. Coach Ezra was not present at the meet, which made it that much more enjoyable. Remember, he was banned from international flights by the National Sports Committee for his drunken episode on an international flight about a year before.

On the flight, the girls, like girls do, were chatting each other's ears off. The subject came up about coach Ezra. This usually took the same course of pointing out how mean he is, but this time it was different. Anna explained, "Nicole came out and started talking how good he is. She never talked like that before. She said how we just don't understand him and if you get to know him he is a really nice person. This is after so many episodes of her coming into our room after being beaten. I couldn't believe it. I never told anyone that he hit me or Nicole. We kept these things to ourselves. But what I could not believe, really, was she admitted to us she was having sex with him." Nicole was sixteen now. "The worst thing she said is that she has been sleeping with him since she was thirteen. Nicole was talking as if they were in love."

Thirteen years old. This means Ezra was thirty at the time. Now how could any girl make a conscious decision to sleep with a grown man at the age of thirteen? How many times was she beaten by him? She didn't tell anyone about these new feelings for Ezra until now. Did she feel this love for him when she was thirteen?

Let us take a second to look at the law of Anna's country. According to the law, if Ezra did have sex with Nicole when she was thirteen then he did break the law of consent, but only by one year. The age of child consent was only fourteen in 1990. Not until recently, in 2002, did the government overwhelmingly vote to raise the age to sixteen.

Laws concerning age are made in regard to maturity. In these matters they take the greatest average of a group's behavior to make the decision whether at this age they are mature enough to engage in the activity in question. Of course, there are those who deviate from the average; some people look and behave much older than they are; conversely, some people are older, but their behavior more immature.

Now let's take a look at Nicole at the age of thirteen. She was far from looking like a physically mature young lady. She had not even yet reached puberty. She was what we call in the Unites States a "late bloomer." At thirteen years of age she was not at all developed sexually and her appearance was not much different than that of a boy of the same age. This was the same case for Anna. She was also a "late bloomer." Both girls at thirteen years of age were skinny, petite, and had no signs of sexual development. Furthermore, according to Anna, at the time of their revealing conversation on the plane back from Argentina when they were sixteen years old, they were still petite, and neither of them had yet started menstruating, let alone physically or sexually develop.

The above is based on technical arguments concerning law. Now let's take a brief moment and look at ethical law. To an American it looks simple: A thirteen-year-old, prepubescent girl who had sex with her thirty-year-old coach brings two things to mind: child molestation and pedophilia. The trust that Ezra built with his swimmers was exploited by him to satisfy his sexual urges. I'm confident to say that Nicole was coerced, molested, and beaten. Furthermore, she was raped; not just physically, but of her dignity. She was afraid to tell others because she felt no one could do anything about it. "Anything" meaning to stop her abuse, bring Ezra to justice, keep her protected, and allow her to keep swimming for her country. In the end, because of a sense of helplessness, she accepted her situation.

Nicole was a sports sweetheart to her country. She was known and loved for standing on the medal platform and competing in national, European, world, and Olympic events. Though she was receiving media attention and the recognition of being a champion, she was at the same time being molested and abused, and no one knew about it, not even her family. No one knew about it because she was too afraid to tell anyone.

11

Other Girls From the Team

I have no doubt that many more girls on the team were molested and abused. In fact, I met many swimmers from Anna's team personally while I was investigating this story in Europe. Of course when I met them with Anna, the subject of molestation was not talked about directly to them, but Anna would always point out which ones were molested after we parted. Understandably, Anna doesn't have the nerve to talk about such treatment with anyone else. For her it's just a bad point in life and there isn't any reason to bring it up since, as she said, "nothing can be done about it anyway." Even Mariana, Anna's mother, didn't know anything about what happened. Anna told me she doesn't want this story out until she finally leaves the country because she would feel ashamed to be around her mother when she finds out. Anna believes her mother will be very upset that she never told her what happened when it did. Mariana knows nothing of what happened even to this day, although she does suspect things.

I'll reiterate what boggles my mind about all of this. Ezra, to this day, the day this book went to print, is still coaching a girl's team in the same city at the same pool at KA-14. Because of this, I always insisted to hear everything that Anna knew about the situation. It really took awhile for her to tell me everything, as she felt insecure of how others would view her once they knew about it, but I had to know all the details before I could write about it. I needed to know how much Ezra really did. The more I could write about, the more I would have the opportunity to protect anyone else who may come into contact with him. Anna really opened up when she knew for sure she would be leaving her country. To back up her own testimony she even tried contacting some of the other girls who were abused. Some of the swimmers who she claimed had been molested were merely acquaintances of hers, while others were good friends throughout her swimming career. Unfortunately, she has been out of contact with most of them for a long time. Anna knew of a few events involving the other girls that

I thought would be wise to write about. Andrea was one of them.

Anna was about sixteen at the time, and Andrea was thirteen. Anna recalls, "There was a small group of us girls talking about the usual gossip of the day after swim training, and there was always something about our coach. Andrea was part of this group. We were talking the usual rumors and how much of a pig Ezra was. Later that day Andrea came to my room, and she wanted to tell me something about the coach. She was a little nervous when she said that one day Ezra called her to his room later in the evening after training. After she walked in, Ezra closed and locked the door behind her. She told me she just stood there afraid because she knew the rumors about Coach Ezra before".

For Andrea, going to the coach's room may have only caused minimal concern due to the gossip she had become accustomed to hearing, but coming into the room and having the coach lock the door, shutting off the only way out, surely raised these concerns to fear. At this point she could only hope that the rumors weren't true, but unfortunately they were.

Anna went on, "He wrapped his arms around her and started kissing her. She said she was too afraid to move. She started crying, then told him to stop and let her out. She started crying louder and kept telling him to let her go. Not until she started crying loud enough where it was possible for others outside the room to hear her did Ezra let her go and opened the door."

Andrea went a step further than the other girls by telling her family what had happened. She was from a good family, and her brother was a policeman. Anna told her that if an investigation took place she would support her. Andrea told her brother what had happened, but the structure of law gave no confidence to anyone, even to her brother. She also said her brother had no power because Ezra was quite a famous swim coach. Instead he thought it better if someone would just kill him.

How could anyone in Anna's country have any confidence that the justice system was protecting good, innocent people after a policeman told him or her that nothing could be done about this? Andrea's brother was a policeman, but felt powerless to do anything. He felt that it was a better idea for someone to take justice into their own hands. If the police do not want to get involved, then where else can people in these situations turn? Who has the power to protect them? What kind of civilized society is this? It's not! Justice only came to the people who had power to enforce their own justice. The girls didn't know anyone like this. Nicole came from a well-off family of two parents who were chemists, but thought it better not to tell them. Andrea had a good family whose brother was a policeman. She and Anna lost all confidence with the justice system, especially when her brother wanted to help but couldn't. These girls felt they had no options, and Ezra was free to do what he wanted without any repercussions.

Without any substantial ramifications Ezra increasingly showed his confident and arrogant behavior. He began to do things even though others could clearly see what was going on. For example, according to Anna, one day at the swimming pool when training had just ended, everyone got out except for a girl named Irena. Everyone started to the showers, and there were only a few swimmers left on the pool deck. Anna was one of them.

"Irena was in the middle of the pool. Ezra jumped in and swam to her. When he got to her, he just grabbed on to her breasts right in front of everyone. You couldn't really see since they were in the middle of the pool, but that's exactly what it looked like. Later, Irena told me that is exactly what happened," Anna.

Even with Nicole, Coach Ezra started to be more open. This made sense, as she was his favorite, and was now over the legal age of consent. Nicole was always showing up with the coach in the morning to practice. Ezra was of course still drinking, but now even more heavily than before. On those days that he didn't show up, the team would ask Nicole if the coach would be there that day or not. Nicole always knew, since she was now sleeping in his apartment in the city most of the time.

Nicole and Coach Ezra's relationship became pretty much out in the open. Anna says: "They looked horrible together. He was older, with a big stomach, balding and out of shape. She was petite, young, and athletic. It just didn't look right." Nicole was given presents by Ezra such as clothes and earrings. She was definitely his favorite, or, as Anna said, "The girl that he could have sex with without giving him so many problems." He knew that everyone on the team knew about the relationship and about some of his other incidents. In his mind at this time, his relationship with Nicole was permitted. He didn't care very much about what others would think. This is made evident by looking at the actions that followed, such as her sleeping with him at his apartment, and them spending most of their free time together. In fact, when Nicole was around sixteen years old, team members would hear them having sex in Ezra's room.

"Twice I heard them having sex when we were on meets. Once we went to Egypt for training. Helena, Erik, and I were coming back from an evening out in the town. We were walking past Ezra's room on the way to ours. It was so loud. We heard Nicole and our coach having sex as if they wanted everyone to hear. We all started laughing and Helena rushed me and Erik to our rooms as if we were too immature for all of this," Anna.

Exemplifying Coach Ezra and Nicole's sexual relationship is not being done to show that sex at their ages is something not acceptable, especially since Nicole was now around seventeen years old and Ezra was about thirty-four. What it does illustrate is the hypocrisy of the coach's rules that he set for the team. He still enforced his rules through punishment as much as he could. The rule concerning boys according to Anna was: never talk to boys and never have a boyfriend. The girls couldn't drink alcohol, go to clubs, or wear any fashionable clothes. These were Ezra's rules, but at the same time he was tempting and coercing his swimmers to break them, but only with him. He offered them alcohol, he was buying Nicole clothes and jewelry, and most despicable of all, he was trying to have sex with many of them while trying to keep them from having sex with anyone else. It looks like he was trying to isolate them for his own purposes. And, as I stated earlier he is still coaching a young girls' team, but who knows what rules he implements now, or how many other girls he is exploiting like this.

12

A Civil Society? More People Know

Anna asserts: "If I would have had a father I would have been protected from this. No one could protect me from the coach." Anna has said this to me again and again. After investigating this story and getting a feel for her country, I do understand her position and how she feels. Our story of a national and Olympic-level coach who had the country's most successful female swimming team is highly unlikely to happen in the United States or any other western European country. The risks for the perpetrator are too high. The public would not stand for it. The judicial system, along with support from private and professional organizations, would act immediately. Victims would not only have support from their parents, but also from the whole community. Even convicts in prison would be waiting for the molester to show up at their prison to show support for the victim. In the United States, prison is the last place you want to be if you are a child molester. Child abusers and molesters are usually separated from other inmates for their own safety. Convicts also want to protect their children on the outside, and knowing there will be one less molester in the world makes them feel their children are that much safer. So why do we in the West think like this?

We believe that regardless of what the law states child molesters in a society simply exploit and damage the psychological and even physical health of children. They damage the psychological health of children because children come to know that our society does not accept such behavior. We don't accept such behavior because manipulating and abusing a child for one's own personal gratification would teach a child that exploiting others is OK. It is not OK to exploit others for your own fun, sexual outlet, or selfishness. If a society tolerated exploiting others, as is the case in Anna's country, then it would be very difficult to use the word civilized to describe that society. This is probably my strongest accusation of the country Anna is from in this book, and it is a justifiable one.

What has been written above not only gives insight of my higher reasons to write this book, it also illustrates the level of justice that the people of Anna's country believe in today: little justice for those who have little power. As Anna stated before, "If I would have had a father I would have been protected from this." She is not talking about her father giving her moral support to go to the police and file a complaint. She has no confidence that justice can be served through the established authority. She means that her father would have had the physical might to end what was happening, even if it took others to help him. This system in which vigilantes provide the only justice illustrates a breakdown in society.

But how can we blame her or any other girl on the team for not voicing what happened? Those who would listen could do little. Thirteen-year-old Andrea told her family and her brother was a policeman. Her brother even said that going through the police would be useless. In a society like this, what is your alternative? Can you get justice, and if so, how?

In 1996 the stories were spreading about the things Coach Ezra was doing. Nicole verified many of the rumors about herself to team members in 1994 on the plane home from Argentina. Around the same time Andrea told her family and Anna about her encounter with the coach molesting her in his room. The suspicion about many more acts involving other team members was very high. Nicole's husband substantiated the claims of other girls by telling me in 2004 that Nicole could write a huge book of all the things she knew about Ezra's abuse. Nicole was very close with Ezra, and surely knew far more than Anna, who was the main source of my information. Another young girl by the name of Maria came on the team later. As the other abused girls had been, she was also prepubescent when she joined the team, according to Anna. Many swimmers and staff believed she was being molested. To them it was the same scenario as Nicole: Ezra was buying gifts for her and she was staying in his room late at night. Everyone said that she was his new favorite after Nicole left the team. According to Anna, a teammate told Maria's parents what everyone suspected. This teammate told Anna that Maria's parents were in denial because they didn't want to hurt either their own or their daughter's chances of having a better life. Then there was another girl, Kristina. Two years after Anna left the team, she went swimming at KA-14 for some exercise. The pool attendant knew Anna well and told her some of the latest gossip. The attendant claimed that on more than one occasion, very early in the morning while it was still dark outside, Ezra came out of his room with Kristina and asked him to unlock the door so he could lead Kristina to a waiting taxi. It is difficult for an American to believe that with this many people suspecting something, some authority didn't get involved. In America the complaints would at least be followed up by the appropriate athletic committee. With parents coming forward, there would be at least a low-key investigation before the story was released to the media. Even if one girl came out about molestation, the authorities would be all over the situation, trying to find out what really happened. But this was not the case in Anna's country. There, justice is ill-served in such cases. For those swimmers who were abused by Ezra, the only hope was that someone would do something about it, and apparently someone did.

One early morning in the summer of 1996 Ezra walked out the door of their hometown training center of KA-14. He immediately found himself surrounded by a few men. In moments he would be unconscious from a severe beating that would almost take his life.

Ezra was in the hospital for many days. His condition was severe. He slipped in and out of a coma three times. He eventually improved and was allowed to have visitors. Anna went to see him.

She recalls: "We thought nothing of it since he often misses training in the morning. We heard what happened from a staff member at KA-14. I hated my coach but I went to see him to be nice. He was unconscious when I first entered. He was balding, so I saw his head all black and blue. He also had a tube going into his stomach." While in the hospital, Ezra was also diagnosed with another major problem: severe pancreas damage due to drinking. He told his swimmers only half the truth, saying that he was there from an alcohol-related medical problem. He never mentioned to Anna during this visit that he was beaten. He missed days upon days of training due to surgery.

Nineteen ninety-six was not entirely bad for Ezra and the team. That year the Summer Olympics were held in Atlanta, Georgia. Anna's childhood dream had come true. She made the team with Nicole. This was the girls' first time in the United States. Their training suffered due to Ezra missing so many sessions and also, according to Anna, his lack of interest. She remembers, "He still missed many days of coaching us due to his drinking even though he got out of the hospital not long ago, and when we were at the Olympic Games, he was out drinking and enjoying the trip like he was a tourist, not being around and advising us on what last minute preparations might be necessary". Neither girl received a medal, but just the thrill and experience of being a competitor felt good. They got to see the city of Atlanta, as Anna met a nice fellow who worked at the Olympic camp who showed her around. She wasn't very impressed, as the American movies she saw at home made it look much better than what is really was. She remembers: "The city was in better shape than mine, but I never felt safe in the night or around poor people. Even my American friend showing me around told me so many places I shouldn't go. This is much different than my country where you could really go anywhere at anytime and not worry about being raped or robbed. But all in all it was a good experience for me. I wish I would have seen more of America, like California."

Looking back on this year, things were really quite volatile for Coach Ezra. He did make it to the Atlanta Olympics with some of his swimmers. Then there were his highly troublesome problems. Some of his female swimmers were obviously concerned enough about what was happening to them to start talking to friends and family. Ezra was beaten almost to death, and he had a major operation due to both his beating and his alcoholism. And, if that wasn't enough, his star swimmer, Nicole, later that year left the team.

13

Leaving the Team

Nicole was Ezra's star, the country's top freestyle swimmer, and a member of the 4×100 combination team. The prestige not just for Ezra's but the country's team took a big blow. It wasn't surprising that Nicole took her opportunity to break away after so much abuse. Her love for Ezra, which she revealed just over a year ago, now didn't look so real after all. Strangely enough, just after the 1996 Olympics, she took a trip to the Croatian resort town of Dubrovnik while recovering from severe depression, no doubt caused by abuse one can only imagine. There she met a local Croat named Sunic who was part of the local government. They became friends and stayed in touch after Nicole went back home. The relationship became serious, and Sunic flew to Nicole's country and stayed there with her a short time. They returned together to Croatia, and soon after that they married and made Dubrovnik their new home. Nicole later began to swim successfully for Croatia.

It wasn't long after Nicole left when another top swimmer under Ezra would soon leave the team. Anna decided at this time that she had also had enough. It was just before the 1997 world championships in Sydney, Australia.

Anna asserts: "I felt like I wasn't getting enough from swimming. I didn't want to be around Ezra anymore. Nicole took her chance to escape it all, and she did. I was hoping for a chance like that. There was more stress than enjoyment and I wasn't improving how I lived. It just wasn't worth it. That sounds bad since I finally made the Olympics and could surely make the next one, but it was true. It could have been much better. If it was better then I would have stayed. Other athletes were going to other countries and finding a better life and better facilities to train. I'm sure in other countries you wouldn't have problems with a coach like we had. I was asked a few times early in my career to join Norway's team, whose coach I knew very well. I almost left but would have felt bad swimming for another country. I think if I was asked later when I was older I would have. When I was young I really didn't want to leave home and my mother. She would have been all alone."

Anna and her mother also had money problems. As an athlete, she was given a government paycheck which was around $100 per month, but this was not nearly enough to live worry free. She began to look for further support and naturally started looking for a husband. The government had a budget to take care of their athletes, but this was yet another area in which her coach was quite unfair. She recalls: "Ezra got money to support the team and all sportsmen and women knew if you made the national team you would surely be supported much better. Ezra used his money to attract swimmers from other cities to join the team. He took care of them, but he didn't do for us what he did for them. I was never given any place or any way of transport while others did. I was never given a car, but never really expected to, but later Nicole was bought one by Ezra. We even had a driver that worked for the team and always took Nicole where she had to go. Unfortunately he rarely took me home even when Nicole was taken that way for school. The coach always tried to make me feel like he was doing me a big favor the few times the driver took me home. The more

Ezra felt you depended on him the more he took advantage of you. We gave at least 25% of our winnings to the coach, which I understand, but we only made about $100 to $2500 if we won a competition. I was approached by one business-man who wanted to sponsor me. When we both met about this with Ezra he told the businessman if he wants to sponsor one person on the team he has to sponsor the whole team. It was more money than [the businessman] wanted to spend, so he didn't. But, Ezra was such a hypocrite since he let sponsors support Nicole and not the rest of the team. I'm sure he got some sort of money from Nicole's sponsors. So it wasn't worth swim-ming for my country anymore because I just came home to what you see now (At the time, Anna was living in a two-room apartment in an old, com-munist-era panelock building)."

Anna explained that financially it wasn't worth it, but that more money would have made living there more bearable. During my visit to Anna's country, I stayed in an apartment that was owned by one of her uncles who was in the same building as Anna. It wasn't much; cozy, with all the neces-sities, but very few luxuries. It may be safe to say that the government money given to Ezra was not justly passed down to all his players. Anna and Nicole did get as much food as they could eat, and they later received the necessary clothes for training, but they never got even a small apartment, though swimmers from different cities did. Throughout her whole swimming career, the only luxury that improved her standard of living was her first telephone. Because of this, Anna began to think about leaving the team. A country can't keep their athletes around too long when they are given so little.

Anna of course could not approach Coach Ezra with all these reasons for leaving the team. Her excuse to him was a small part of her overall motive, but it was true and simple. "When I talked to Ezra about this he really tried to get me to stay. I told him that I wanted a family. That was the reason I gave him. I did want a family, but not right now. I even seriously thought about joining another country's team. My coach was talking to me like he knew why I was leaving. He was saying that I just needed a man since I have been training for so long and never really had a boyfriend. I did have a boyfriend at this time, but he didn't know. It is like he still didn't want to understand what I was saying. He then told me

I just need to have sex, and that I should have it with him since all the other girls on the team do. He said that almost all girls sleep with the coach for better results. That is exactly what he told me," Anna.

He admitted to Anna he was sleeping with all the other girls on the team. Neither I nor Anna would go so far as to claim he was really sleeping with all of them even though he suggested this himself, but in this discussion he showed his arrogance as well as his motives. For Anna, the main reason she was leaving the team in the first place was the coach's abuse and the urges to have sex with his swimmers that he couldn't keep under control.

He was able to admit he was sleeping with his swimmers without any fear of what this may have implied. He set out rules to keep his female swimmers away from potential boyfriends in order to increase his own chances of having sex with them. He showed this by telling Anna about his belief that she wanted to leave the team because she wanted to have sex. Why would he think this? Did he think that being on his team made girls feel sexually suppressed? If what I have written so far is true, then sexual suppression was surely an ulterior motive for Ezra's behavior.

Though it was shocking and very disrespectful for Ezra to tell her this, it just proved what Anna and the other swimmers had thought: that, as she said, "If he could, he would have slept with every girl on the team."

She made her decision to leave final. Sadly enough, her last swim meet took place this year at the 1997 European championships in Goteborg, Sweden. Along with her 2nd place in the team's 4×100 medley, she again broke her country's record in the 100 meter breast stroke, which she herself held, taking first place. She was her country's top and one of the world's leading female breast stroke swimmers, but that wasn't enough to keep her doing what she wanted to be doing most of all—swimming for her country.

Within a year both girls left the team at the height of their game, taking with them the greater talent and prestige of Ezra's and the nation's female team. Ezra would not have female swimmers like them again. Nicole was eighteen and Anna nineteen when they ended their careers. They never represented their country in sports again. As young as they were at this point there is no doubt they would have gone further and achieved more. This is what they truly wanted, but only one of them, Nicole, was motivated to enter the pool again.

14

Steroid Scandal

Ezra's life took another wrong turn after Anna and Nicole left, this time in the form of a much-publicized scandal involving the use of performance-enhancing drugs. Such drugs are so common in sports that it is very difficult to eradicate them completely. Steroids and other drugs are so pervasive in sports that there are even some who argue that we should just allow them. Of course, allowing this type of activity creates the argument that if people do something enough, it should be legalized. Should we, following the same argument, allow littering, drinking and driving, graffiti, stealing, and rape? Of course not. The argument against steroids in sports such as swimming basically exists to "let us have the best athlete win, not the best chemist." In sports there is widespread cheating, and it comes not just from those who are getting busted, but also from the top athletes who are undetected and go on to win. The saying I use to describe the mentality of such cheaters in sports is, "Even though I'm not a champion, I can make it appear that I am the champion." Because of this mentality, we see those who follow the rules lose, and those who break them win. It's just not fair.

We must also take a look at the incentives for winning. The winners get sponsors and endorsements; basically a lot of money. Unfortunately, in any sport where speed and endurance is needed, there will be abuse of performance-enhancing drugs, especially when money is involved. American pro football is a prime example. Multi-million dollar contracts are given to the players who have the most speed, strength, and endurance; all of which are characteristics that can be greatly enhanced by drugs such as steroids. There are few people who believe American football is not completely saturated.

In international sports, such as the games we commonly see in the Olympics, there are the same motivations to use performance-enhancing drugs, because these sports provide athletes the incentive to live more comfortable lives. Good athletes in most countries are at least paid for the necessities of living, while other countries lavish expensive gifts upon their sports stars. Those are two ultimate incentives for cheating: the feeling of being a champion, and financial gain.

The sport of swimming is no stranger to the use of steroids or the incentives to use them. A few thousand dollars can be made in some swim meets, along with governmental support money, and all the perks from endorsements. Swim coaches usually take a percentage of the team members' winnings, so it would seem that not just the athletes are motivated to cheat. In the past, there have been cases where there was systematic governmental support for cheating, which allowed the athletes little choice; they simply had to use steroids or not be on the team. This was demonstrated by the famous East German doping program that was carried out under the protection of the East German government. At the 1976 Summer Olympic swimming events in Montreal, the East German female swim team won all but 2 gold medals. The funny thing is that before this happened, only one German had ever won a gold medal in Olympic swimming history. A scandal erupted, and a later investigation uncovered the whole program.

Due to out-of-control drug use, doping controls were implemented in most international sports, but they still need to be perfected. Major steps have been taken, yet there are still those who are caught, and of course there are governments that are highly suspected of having hidden government-sanctioned programs. China is today's major suspect. Since the 1990s, China has been the nation caught the most by doping controls in international competitions. In fact, from the time that doping controls were implemented until the year 2000 China had the highest number of swimmers with positive test results or caught in possession of enhancement drugs with 28 cases, while Russian and Soviet swimmers were second, having only 6 cases.

Of former Soviet drug-enhancing cases four were from a January 1998 doping test at a training camp in Moldova. Four swimmers, 2 male and 2 female, were found with the steroid oxandrolone in their system along with the masking agent furesemide, which was used to hide the steroids from doping control. These swimmers all had the same coach: Ezra.

When multiple athletes from one country are caught by doping control, suspicion is not just put on those athletes but also attention is directed towards their coaches and those above them. This makes it very embarrassing for a country when the athletes who represent the nation are caught cheating. This embarrassment led Anna's country to undertake an investigation surrounding Coach Ezra.

The interesting things about this case were the way in which the investigation was handled and the final judgment from the world governing body for swimming, FINA. To learn about the investigation itself one really needs to read the testimonies, investigation, and interviews that appeared in the news sources. According to the final summarization of the event, just before the trip to Moldova a girl from Ezra's team came to practice one day with chocolate for everyone to eat. In the chocolate this girl had hidden the steroids so all the other players wouldn't know it. So, this young girl took all the blame. The punishment that was handed out by FINA for the 4 swimmers who had the drugs in their system was a two-year ban for each of them. Coach Ezra had no blame in the matter.

Anna has a very revealing story about this event. She told me that if she had said anything about the matter at the time others on her team would be quite upset. "It was like showing the team's dirty underwear." Anna said. But she told it to me later in order to show another side of Ezra.

"I heard that members of my former team were in trouble for using anabolics from the news. I just left the team not long before. I thought nothing about it but it wasn't a surprise. I really never even thought I took steroids until maybe the last year of my swimming career in 1996. Around 1996 Ezra started putting us on a vitamin program that was made up of many pills. I was always interested in my training— how we ate, trained, etc. I was into fitness so I wanted this later after my swimming career in case I swam for another country or became some sort of swimming coach myself. When Ezra gave us these pills and the schedule to eat them I wrote this in my journal and drew what they looked like. My journal is like my diary and I wrote all sorts of stuff in it. Ezra never told us what each pill exactly was and what it did. He just said they were vitamins, but I'd never seen these kind before. I actually can't say if they were steroids or not, but they didn't look anything like the vitamins you can buy at the store. These were different colors and very small. I never told anyone about this because I thought maybe these could be something like anabolics.

"Then one day when Nicole and I were staying together in the same room she found my journal and read it. She saw that I was writing down everything about the pills, so she took it to Ezra. I can't believe she did that. I was so mad. It became a scandal with the coach. He was yelling at me, saying 'do you want to give this to another team or something?' So I got yelled at, that was all.

"I knew later in [1996] that we were doing something sneaky, even if it wasn't doing steroids. We were at the 1996 Regional Championship in Moldova. I can't remember if it was a day before or a couple days before the competition but the coach said 'C'mon, let's go get our blood cleaned.' We all went to a small clinic— [it was] only about a three-story-tall building. We all went into a room and lay down on the beds. We all got a needle in our arm with a tube. I think we laid there with the IV dripping in the tube for about 1 or 2 hours. It was long. It made us have to pee badly. That was all. We just left after that. But, after team members the next year got caught with steroids in their system with something to hide them, then it makes me think that in 1996 in Moldova we probably were doing the same thing. I don't know if the team went back to the same clinic or not," Anna.

This was quite interesting, and would have been very helpful to FINA's investigation committee in the 1998 Moldova incident, but that is not the most revealing thing Anna had to say about the matter.

"Ezra called me sometime soon after his swimmers were caught in Moldova. He wanted to meet me somewhere and have a talk. He didn't tell me exactly why. When we met he asked me if I knew about what had happened in Moldova and I said yes. He said that we need someone to take the blame for this because he can't do it. He asked if I would say that I gave the swimmers steroids. I said no. He asked if I would do it because it would be too much for him and he may be fired and lose his national team. He would be banned for this and maybe for a long time since he was the coach. But I wasn't going to take the blame. I told him again that I won't do it. He said we can tell them something like you put it in chocolate and gave it to the team. He was pleading with me and I still said no. He ended by saying, 'I'll give you a couple of days to think about this.' I told him it was time for me to leave. He said he would call me in a few days and I just said, 'alright.'

"He did call me a few days later like he said. He wanted to meet with me again, but this time I took my boyfriend, Milan, since last time I felt really uncomfortable. I'm glad Milan was with me because he really helped out. I went inside the cafe where Ezra was and had Milan wait outside. Ezra asked again if I would take the blame. I said no, I'm not going to do this. He then tried to bribe me by saying he would give me three months of lieutenant's pay plus pay me lieutenant's monthly salary for the next two or three years and I don't have to work. Still I said no. He then got upset and wanted me to come with him. He wanted to talk with me more in a room upstairs. I just wanted to leave and there was no way I would have gone with him but since Milan was there I thought it would be OK. So I got Milan from outside and I saw that Ezra didn't like this. We followed him upstairs and walked into a room where there was a man in a suit with a brief case and some papers on the table. He was standing behind the table and asked if we would sit down.

We sat at the table and he started saying, 'When did you put the drugs in the chocolate? When did you give it to the team?' I was in shock. I couldn't believe the coach tried to frame me like this. I just sat with my eyes wide open and frozen. I started to cry a little as I could not believe I was in such a position. I am so glad that Milan was with me because he told this guy to wait a moment. Then asked, 'What chocolate?' and 'What drugs are you talking about?' This guy could see that Milan wasn't stupid and wouldn't sit still like I did. So Milan took my hand and we got up. Milan finally said 'If you have any questions for her you have to bring permission from the police next time.' So we left, and I was so glad to be out of there. I just went home and cried, as I really felt that it was like a final knife my coach put in me. Who could like a man like this? He only cares about himself," Anna.

So, Anna refused to take the coach's blame for giving his swimmers steroids without their knowledge. The ones who ended up being banned from swimming were the swimmers themselves while Coach Ezra got off by placing the blame on some young female swimmer. Of course the papers didn't report this, because no one wanted to talk about it. I'm confident that FINA surely would have appreciated hearing such testimony from Anna.

Anna told me that her reputation would have been severely smeared if she had taken the blame. She finished swimming a month before this, and ended with a successful but short career that she could be proud of. The upsetting thing is that the word got around that Anna was the culprit. She felt that Ezra had already been starting rumors before he approached her later to try to place the blame for the doping scandal on her.

Unfortunately, there are probably still many who think that Anna is the one who gave drugs to her former teammates because of the rumors Ezra spread. A year later, an older coach who was involved in swimming asked her why she took the blame when everyone knew she was innocent. She told him the real story and he wasn't surprised. Another example involves a former teammate of Anna's named Petra. She was three years younger than Anna. In one of her college classes she was learning about the use of drugs in sports. To her surprise, when the professor was talking about doping, they used Anna as an example, saying that she was the person who put the steroids in the chocolate in the 1998 scandal. Petra and all the other swimmers on the team at the time knew that Ezra had tried to put the blame on Anna before putting it on some other girl. Petra held a lot of respect for Anna. She told the professor and class that she had swum on the same team as Anna and that the story was false. She also told them that Anna had nothing to do with it and that the rumors were all to get the blame off the coach.

A few years after her country's steroid scandal, a reporter approached Anna with the desire to do a big story on Ezra. Anna was thinking about not just giving the reporter the story of how Ezra tried to use her as the patsy, but also about his molestation of team members. After thinking for a few days, she declined giving any story at all out of fear for her and her mother's own well-being.

With all this in mind, it appears that Ezra was the one giving steroids to his team. His vitamin program, his taking the team to get their blood cleaned, and his pleading for Anna to take the blame when his swimmers tested positive for drugs all support this theory. Maybe he was part of a bigger program, who knows? Unfortunately, his swimmers are the ones who paid for it all.

Also unfortunate is the injustice that many believe Anna is the person who was behind it all. It is equally distressing that this story was being used at Petra's sports institute where many other people were surely told the incorrect story. The problem may be that once the story had circulated for a while people lost interest even when the papers later reported as a minor story that they had found the girl who was really responsible. I think it would be better reported as, "The girl who finally agreed to take the blame, thanks to Ezra's persuasion." The damage was already done to Anna. It is the same situation as when the dominant media reports a story, then weeks later puts an apologetic correction on the back page—like anyone really pays much attention to those. Anna always wanted to write about her experiences and get the story out about Ezra, but she never felt safe while living in her country. Then, while on vacation in Prague, she met me.

Part 2

15

From Meeting Anna to Starting the Story

Meeting Anna while she was on vacation in the Czech Republic was just another string of fate. I took interest in her physical attraction, personality, and also her disturbing story. What I thought would be a couple meetings with her turned into us spending most of her two weeks vacation in Prague together. Besides enjoying her company, I was also trying to talk her into giving this story to someone who would write about it. She had always wanted to, but never felt comfortable enough to do it. At the time I met her, she was set on leaving her country. Maybe that is why she decided to tell me.

I was on summer break from my University and thought I could help this along. I thought maybe I could do this myself. Maybe I could write a short article about the gist of what happened and give it to a newspaper. I had no experience in this field, but I was willing to try. I probably wouldn't be so motivated if the story wasn't so current and affecting innocent children. What kept tugging at my soul was that Ezra was still coaching. This just had to stop.

For the time being, although I had thoughts of acting in some way to get this story to the public, I just enjoyed my time with lovely Anna. After a couple of days in romantic Prague together I could see that Anna was trying to get closer to me. This was fabulous! Such a soft–spoken, beautiful lady she was. She had blonde hair and green eyes, with a body that was still in top shape. Even with all of that, it was the simple way she carried herself that I really found attractive. She could have dressed in high-fashion clothing and been decorated by the richer men of the world if she had wanted to, but that didn't seem to interest her. She was just looking for a good man to start a family with. Unfortunately, as I was not finished with school and far away from my real home in Las Vegas I wasn't in a position to help her with that.

Our time together became heated and passion-ate. Our first kiss was just before sunset on the famous Charles Bridge in sight of Prague Castle that rests just a short distance on top of one of the tallest hills in Prague. She made me want to leave everything I had in Prague behind. I almost did at a point. It just wasn't my time, and I regret it now.

Her two-week vacation seemed like two days. Anna returned to her country, but for the last half of her stay I brought a notepad along with me everywhere we went, and jotted down everything she had to say about her ordeal. Her walking through the passport gate at Prague's Ruzne airport was not the last time I would see her. We kept in touch by email and phone calls. We both wanted to see each other, and she was trying more to take our relationship to the next level. I decided I would visit her when I would be on school break next summer, not just to see her, but also to find out more about Ezra. As I gathered more information, my investigative article started turning into a short story.

16

Getting Her to Act

Summer break came and I was so excited to go to another country and see Anna. I flew from Prague to the capital of Anna's country. Anna took a train from her city and met me at the airport. She held a big smile for me at the bottom of the escalator I was riding down to meet her. It was nighttime, and I could only see some of the lit-up buildings on our taxi ride to the train station. We took a pre-dawn train back to her city. I didn't get to see much of the country as I slept during the whole six-hour ride. As we pulled into her city everything was just like she had explained. It was not as nice as the capital, and everything was in need of repair. The train station was about the only new thing in the city besides the cafés springing up in the center. They were in the middle of taking out the ugly pavement sidewalks in some parts of town and replacing them with the same beautiful brick that had been used in Prague.

The Cathedral, which stood near the river with its golden domes, was the definite sparkle of the city.

We took a bus along the broken-up street right to her apartment building, which was still on Afinska Street. Her mother met us as politely as could be with some salads, meat, cheese, and bread on the table. Their kitchen was so small that it was impossible to fit all four chairs around the table, as one side had to go against the wall. It was a two-room apartment with a living room that had been converted into a bedroom for her mother. It was little and modest.

I didn't have a long stay, so starting the next day during breakfast we started talking about her former coach. Anna so much wanted to take me on a tour of her city and told me to just bring my notepad again. It was summer. We first went to see her old swimming pool. When we entered KA-14 Anna was staring at me smiling. Then she directed her eyes up at the wall above the reception desk to see if I noticed something. There were about a half-dozen or so framed photographs of all the former famous swimmers who had trained there hanging on the wall. Anna was among those in the pictures. We then took the stairs up to the main swimming facility. Here, at poolside, I first saw Coach Ezra. He looked just as she had described—a simple-looking, balding man with a large stomach, and as Anna had said, he was still coaching young female swimmers. Just looking at the young girls in the pool and then at him made me sick. Everything at KA-14 looked just like the old photographs Anna had shown to me. Anna noticed a friend of hers on the deck and went to say hello. I stayed standing inside on the stairs, and kept looking out the window. She talked to her friend for about two or three minutes, and then came back without saying anything to Ezra, which was easy to understand. She told me that when they see each other they sometimes just acknowledge the other's presence with a small, monotone "hi;" no facial expression, nothing more.

We left, and just seeing Ezra coaching that team made me very much want to get as many details about this story as I possibly could. My three-week stay would be dedicated to finding out all that I could.

After getting the main part of the story, I tried to figure out what to do with it. First I tried to get Anna to find some sort of organization or at least someone in a position of power who would champion this cause. She thought it would fall on deaf ears and didn't know of any such organizations. I tried to get her to write an anonymous letter and send it out to newspapers, government offices, and her country's athletic committee. She, like many people who lived in a post-Communist system, thought that any such action would be useless. In fact, there is an actual psychological syndrome called post-communist syndrome, one of the characteristics of which is the feeling and attitude that it's useless to try to change anything, especially if you are going against someone in a more powerful position.

I knew that something could be done about this situation, and must. The least I could do was to start talking with friends and people I met to get the word out. I did this every time I had the chance when I was in Anna's city. I can remember every time in a pub, restaurant, or café that people were unnerved when I told them the story. What gave me hope that I could change something was the fact that everyone I talked to was sincerely concerned, shocked, angered, and disgusted by Anna's story. They all admitted this was something terrible, but even though they felt this way, not one of them ever asked what Anna did about it, as if they already knew what the answer would be. I'm sure they felt the same way she did— disgusted that something like this could happen, but helpless to do anything about it.

That was the attitude of Anna's countrymen and women at this time in regard to the sexual abuse and child molestation I've described so far. When the things I have written about happen there, perpetrators and exploiters have little fear of repercussion either by the authorities or the common citizens. It seems that the only time something is done about a crime in Anna's country is when a criminal is caught in the act, and even then it isn't certain whether the police will take action or whether it will be handled by the vigilantes. What gives me the feeling things will change is that the soul of Anna's people is there; They are just like any other people. I believe we know innately through nature and nurture that such things as child molestation, pedophilia, and rape are crimes against the good of humanity. "We" in this case meaning any member of Western society. Anna's country is improving itself after a long, suppressive twentieth century. It had been under the Marxist-influenced yoke of communism which had held it from many positive, progressive social and technological changes. It has recently thrown off this yoke and is making a strong effort to jump back on board with its Western brothers and sisters. Communism tried to split the Western world and failed. Issues still linger, but the burden of grudges and disagreements involving Western cultures are now easier mended. There are bridges being made due to the government's agreement to come to terms, communicate and actively listen to other governments. It is essential for former Soviet countries to improve their social standards and pick up where they left off before the Bolsheviks and Communists came to power. It's necessary for progression on a social and governmental level to be promoted more in Anna's country, and I see this taking place already, though far more needs to be done.

I give great credit to Anna's country and spirit. Their national pride is strong, but not on the arrogant level. They have an intelligent population. They have natural resources, forests, and farmland. It is all there—everything a nation needs to make itself great. To reinforce their spirit they have a rich history of victories and tragedies.

They have a strong sense of identity that has been forged by social upheaval and war. Many older Americans may describe former Soviet nations as "enemies that cannot be trusted." This sentiment is understandable, but this is a new era, and people with this attitude should remember that before they were our enemies they were our friends and that we share genes with many of the hardworking immigrants who came from these countries.

The Communist era was a terrible one. The Soviets were seen as the aggressor because, at times, they were the aggressor. Communism is now reevaluating itself, and since Stalin's rule, every Soviet and Russian leader has taken steps to rid the world of the wrongs of Communism. For example, Khrushchev expressed his greatest accomplishment in his own words with the statement, "The fear is gone." This was his contribution. From then on Brezhnev to Putin led Russians, and in many ways former Soviet countries, down the bumpy road and back on the path with the West. As for Russia's current president, Putin, I cannot say enough good things about this man. In fact, in a 2002 poll he was voted by Europeans as the most-liked president in the world.

The president of Anna's country has also given them something to be proud of. He has all but rid the country of the high-level mafia that robbed the nation of much of its wealth. The country's economy is growing. People there are traveling and seeing more of the world than ever before. The police state is no longer there. There is an optimistic face on the people. Anna's government is establishng good policies for politics and society. It will have to be stronger in a country where criminal elements are deeply embedded and social structure has allowed such acts as exploitation and violence to go unchecked. But like everything else, all things take time.

Although this country is moving in a better direction, there is still little confidence on the part of those like Ezra's former swimmers to come out and demand justice. But look at Anna: she now has the courage to get the story out. She now feels she has an opportunity. She may have built the courage because she now knows she will no longer live in her country, but she is not just running away. With the confidence that she will be protected by living in a different European country, she, at least will tell her story in hopes to change her own country, unlike the others on her team who just left and didn't help when they now have a chance. I hope she is the first of many who can stand up and demand a change for those who have been abused like her and her teammates. We must also think about those who are not such high-profile citizens. Who knows how many stories about common people are out there that need to be addressed. How many other children is this happening to? To move forward and be viewed as a stable and just society Anna's country must tackle this problem. As for our story, it probably would never have reached the public if I hadn't written about it. As for something being done because of what I have written, only time will tell; But Anna and I are confident that someday something will be done, and that those who have been abused will speak out, demand justice, and finally get it.

17

What I Have Done

After my efforts, Anna still didn't have the confidence to tell anyone with influence or authority to take notice of her situation and possibly do something to prevent it from happening again. She didn't want to really let anyone know until she was living in another country. Although I kept bugging her to at least write a letter to someone or maybe contact a reporter, she just couldn't get motivated. As she would always say, "no one here was going to do anything." I could understand why she wouldn't do anything, but this didn't quell my desire to try. My first plan was to write a letter myself. I did this, and sent it out to three different organizations in her country, including the Olympic Committee. Not one of them responded to me. I wanted to find a news reporter right before I left her country and give him the full story in hopes he would investigate, cause attention, and make something happen. Anna knew a good one who wanted to do a story about her a few years ago on the steroid scandal, but when I finally bought my ticket to leave, Anna got cold feet because she wasn't going to leave her country yet. Her excuse was that until she was gone for sure, she didn't want to say anything, and "it was not going to make a difference anyways." I didn't believe that then, and I still don't. When all else failed, I had to try to get her story out myself.

I decided to take it to an American audience. I hoped that in doing so, someone with authority would take notice. Maybe some news agency would look further into it and cause some sort of reaction for the better.

After my stay in Anna's country, my short story turned into a small book. While returning to the United States, I stopped in Prague to take care of a few personal matters. Within two weeks in Prague, I had about eighty pages written. While there, I relayed the story to my friend John, my former Philosophy professor from the University of New York/Prague with whom I was staying. He was amazed by the story and agreed that there would be a huge scandal if something like this were to happen in the United States. A couple days later, he relayed the story to another former student of his. This student then relayed it to his own stepfather, who was coincidentally a well-known reporter and had worked for various newspapers from around the world. His name was Jeremy McKinnon. Jeremy was a true Irishman, with the accent and all the drinking songs that went with it. He was on his way to Prague for his stepson's college graduation, and was excited to meet me and hear more of the story. We met at a nice pub on Manesova Street to discuss things. Jeremy thought we definitely had a story, and contacted a friend who worked in the business of breaking such stories to the proper newspapers and tabloids. To get a story out, we needed to have corroborating evidence to get the papers to take it. As I already stated, we tried to get supporting statements from a few girls, but the ones we thought would help didn't want to get involved. Then we decided that the best thing to do was to try to go to Croatia and get the story from Nicole herself. I asked Anna to call Nicole, and she did. Unfortunately, Anna was too timid to ask Nicole questions over the phone, so she only stated that I was coming out to ask some things about Ezra. Even Jeremy thought this was going to be a long shot since Nicole was preparing herself for her last Olympics in Athens. If she hadn't let this story out yet, then she probably wouldn't want it out now.

I flew down to Croatia one week later and made it to Dubrovnik by train. I stayed in a rather inexpensive hotel right on the beach. It was a nice place that didn't have air conditioning and the summer weather was hot as usual. Nicole came to the hotel with her husband Sunic and I met them at the hotel's outside restaurant. I was a bit nervous to ask Nicole anything in front of him because I didn't know if he knew about the abuse. When I started to tell her that I was there to get information on things that Anna had said about their former coach, her husband stopped me. He said, he had a feeling that I was coming down to specifically ask questions about Ezra's past treatment and that Nicole had nothing to say about the matter. He wasn't rude, but firm. He even asked me if I had a recorder in my bag, which I had placed on the table. I told them that I found it hard not to do anything about the situation when this kind of person was still coaching young girls. Her husband tried to convince me that I should just enjoy my life and not worry about the problems of others since no one could do anything about them. He also said it would cause Nicole and her family too much stress having to deal with all this in the public light. At this time Nicole's parents were living in Dubrovnik and they still didn't know anything about the abuses. Anna told me Nicole's parents had never liked Ezra for some reason. Anna always believed that Nicole's parents suspected something.

I said that I understood everyone's situation, but that I could not let someone like this get away without people knowing about the crimes, especially while the coach was still training others. Nicole's husband seemed to be the only one speaking as Nicole just sat there looking a bit uncomfortable. I relayed to them some of what I had heard and they told me that it was very little compared to what Nicole knew about other events. This of course got me very interested and I wanted to know more, but I knew that they wouldn't tell me much. Her husband continued saying that maybe someday when both Nicole and Anna were older they could write a book together, and if they wrote the book, it would be huge because of all the bad things Nicole knew about Ezra. They would curse Ezra's name and say what a horrible man he was, but they would not give me many more details than the ones I had already written about. One sure thing is that both of them knew far more than what I had written and what Anna knew.

I told them that I couldn't believe they had an opportunity to bring this man to light and let everyone know what he was doing. I could see that Nicole was feeling a bit ashamed because she knew she had a chance to do something, but Sunic seemed more concerned about not letting the public know than she did. I almost felt that if I had been alone with Nicole I could have convinced her to help. I told them I already had people just waiting for a statement from Nicole and that her story would be in the papers in just a couple days, but Sunic was more concerned with his and Nicole's gains and comfort now. This seemed very selfish to me, so I asked, "How do you feel about everyone else who had been abused and those who are most likely being abused more or less like what happened to your wife?" Her husband said not to worry about them and that it would pass and that I should just go enjoy my life. I guess I could do that if I didn't care about anyone else. I guess I could if I didn't have a child of my own that I didn't want to protect from predators of the lowest kind. I could only tell them that I wouldn't do anything before the Athens Olympics the following summer, but that I could not allow myself to sit and do nothing.

Before we parted, we spent a good half hour talking about all sorts of things, but I felt the whole time that her husband was just trying to make me feel good about just letting things go. Unfortunately their talk of success, money, and their better lifestyle only made me more desperate to get the story out, regardless of what they said. They have it much better than most people and could now care less about anyone else who went through the same things as Nicole. How could she just turn away when she knew that others just like her had been and very possibly still were being molested, beaten, and coerced into things they don't want to do?

I stayed my courteous self and we enjoyed each other's company, though we knew that we each had our own intentions. We parted as friends with the usual promises people make without planning to uphold of maybe visiting each other. The next day her husband dropped off some shirts he wanted to give me and Anna. They read, "Enjoy Dubrovnik!!"; and there was a picture of Nicole on them above the phrase, "Nicole Soustruzhnikova World Champion." I think they forgot to put "of swimming" below it, because real champions are made up of much more than that. I was building even more respect for Anna since she seemed to be the only true champion behind this story.

I came away with shirts, but no signed statements to back up Anna's claims. I did come away with more determination, because that's what I needed to finish writing this story. Jeremy McKinnon, the reporter, knew right, it had been a long shot. We didn't get to publish the story through the press, but he told me I needed to write a book and get it finished as soon as possible.

I obviously did get my book done, though I could have published it sooner. I did make a promise to Nicole and Sunic, and that was to not get this story out before Nicole's last Olympics in Athens as to save her much stress from the press so that she could concentrate on training. I did keep that promise. In fact I waited longer than I should have. If this were a story about an American swimmer I wouldn't need to wait, but I also wouldn't need to write it, because once someone knows about a situation like this in the

States it doesn't take long before the police are involved and the media are all over it. Now I can only hope that the people of Anna's country will do something about this.

This story happened not too long ago. Nothing came about from my and Anna's relationship. We still stay in touch with each other. She is grateful that I championed her story and is still helping me do what I can to get it in the open. Just before the completion of this book, Anna met a man from Scotland. She recently married him in her home country and moved just after the wedding to live with him in Scotland. She has no intentions of returning to live in her country. She still loves her home and calls me whenever her country is playing mine in some big sporting event. She roots for her native country's team unconditionally, but says she'd rather die a pub waitress in Scotland than live in such a country as her native one, where she has given so much but gotten back so little.

In November of 2005, Anna went back to visit her mother in her hometown at the same place they have always lived on Afinska Street. During her visit, she was asked to come down to KA-14 for a swimming meet of young teams. She agreed. There she met a friend from her old team, Kristina, whom I've already mentioned. Kristina was now training swimmers of her own at KA-14. During one of the races, she pointed out to Anna one of the young girls. Kristina said with obvious meaning, "that is his new favorite."

To Anna's surprise, she was asked to give the awards to the swimmers on the medal stand. Anna sent me the picture of her awarding these medals. The photo of her giving these awards is just like the black and white photo she gave me of her and Nicole receiving medals from someone many years ago as children on that same stand at KA-14. Anna told me she felt like nothing has changed. Even her old coach, Ezra, was still standing there.